A Parent's Guide to Gifted Teens:

Living with Intense and Creative Adolescents

by Lisa Rivero

Great Potential Press®

A Parent's Guide to Gifted Teens: Living with Intense and Creative Adolescents

Edited by: Jennifer Ault
Interior Design: The Printed Page
Cover Design: Hutchison-Frey

Published by Great Potential Press, Inc.
P.O. Box 5057
Scottsdale, AZ 85261

Printed and bound in the United States of America using partially recycled paper.

Great Potential Press and associated logos are trademarks and/or registered trademarks of Great Potential Press, Inc.

14 13 12 11 10   5 4 3 2 1

At the time of this book's publication, all facts and figures cited are the most current available. All telephone numbers, addresses, and website URLs are accurate and active; all publications, organizations, websites, and other resources exist as described in this book; and all have been verified as of the time this book went to press. The author(s) and Great Potential Press make no warranty or guarantee concerning the information and materials given out by organizations or content found at websites, and we are not responsible for any changes that occur after this book's publication. If you find an error or believe that a resource listed here is not as described, please contact Great Potential Press.

Library of Congress Cataloging-in-Publication Data

Rivero, Lisa.
  A parent's guide to gifted teens : living with intense and creative
adolescents / by Lisa Rivero.
      p. cm.
  Includes bibliographical references.
  ISBN 978-0-910707-99-2
1. Gifted children—Education (Middle school)—United States. 2. Gifted
children—Education (Middle school)—United States—Evaluation. 3. Gifted
children—Counseling of (Middle school)—United States. I. Title.
  LC3993.2.R59 2010
  371.95'73—dc22
                                        2010003790

ISBN 978-0-910707-99-2

Contents

Acknowledgements

This book has been a long time in the making and has seen many changes of direction. Yet somehow, the final text seems to be just what it was always meant to be, due in no small part to the patience and encouragement of Jim Webb and Janet Gore and the talents of everyone at Great Potential Press, including Jennifer Ault and Kristina Grant-Reid. Thank you, as well, to Julee Hutchison and Lisa Liddy for transforming a virtual manuscript into a beautiful book.

The teens I have known and worked with, both informally and in the classroom, are my continual inspiration and give me much hope for the future. Thank you for risking to ask the tough questions of yourselves and others and for sharing of yourselves so generously.

Finally, on a more personal level, I am ever grateful to my family for being there always, especially when I've needed them the most. To Al, whom I continue to admire more than any other person I know. And to Albert, for your exceptional courage, creativity, and caring and who, without writing a word, could be credited with co-authoring this book.

Chapter 1

Introduction

Are you experiencing stress with a gifted teen in your family? Do the intensity, sensitivity, and self-absorption seem different from what you see in other teens? Do you sometimes wonder what is going on with your moody teen who refuses to communicate?

Or do you perhaps have young gifted children and wonder what you can do to support them as they reach adolescence? You know what giftedness looks like in the early years, but you are unsure of what changes to expect, if any, once your children reach middle school and high school ages, especially since gifted programming in your school district stops after eighth grade, and most advice about meeting the social-emotional needs of the gifted is meant for younger children.

Do you have a teen who was never identified as gifted, but now you are wondering if her sensitivity and intensity are somehow connected to her being really smart? What you thought was the usual exuberance of young children now seems qualitatively different from other adolescents, and your daughter suddenly feels out of place, pressured by her friends to dumb down and care more about boys and less about learning.

Does your pre-adolescent child sometimes seem much older than his years—both intellectually and in terms of moodiness—while other days behaving like a typical 10-year-old? Although you know that he is working well beyond his age in academic subjects, you may have assumed that he would follow the "normal" developmental stages of other children his age. However, his development seems to be a mixed bag, alternating between moments of surprising maturity and childish behaviors.

Are you struggling with how best to support your highly gifted teenager, unsure of whether letting her make her own decisions might prevent her from fulfilling her potential? As college application season approaches, you notice her missing deadlines and not applying herself as you think she should. When do support and encouragement become pressure and over-involvement? If you don't step in and take some serious control over planning her future, won't she drift into mediocrity and underachievement?

Maybe you are tired of the entire game of high-stakes testing, competitive parenting, and "education for success" at all costs. You wonder if there is another way to approach the teenage years. Or you might be considering alternative education such as homeschooling for high school. You don't want to ignore the giftedness in your child, but you also don't want others to use it as a way to limit his choices and self-concept.

If any of these situations sounds familiar, then this book is written for you, whether you think of your child as *intense, gifted, creative, driven, talented,* or just *unusually smart.* It is written for anyone with a teenager who fits at least two of these descriptions:

- Is highly sensitive
- Is highly emotional—more so than other adolescents
- Is an intense learner either in focus or scope
- Has great personal energy
- Is perfectionistic
- Is internally driven
- Is highly imaginative
- Doesn't like to be bored
- Converses easily with adults
- Has friendships with adults
- Sometimes has a hard time relating to age peers
- Is reading, thinking, or learning at a level well beyond his or her age in one or more subject areas
- Has ability levels that are all over the place—high in some areas and not in others
- Is extremely mature in some areas or on some days and remarkably childlike at other times

In Chapter 2, we will learn more about giftedness—how to understand it, how to recognize it, and how it affects families. For now, though, the important point is that giftedness is not just being book smart or good at school. Yes, many gifted children do excel in school, learn easily and rapidly, and readily show their abilities on standardized tests. However, there is much more to being gifted than academic honors or other public recognition. In fact, many gifted children and teens are not at the top of their class and don't collect honors and awards or go to prestigious schools. And they shouldn't necessarily be expected to.

Growing a Book: Lessons from Homeschooling

A Parent's Guide to Gifted Teens is not about homeschooling, although our family's 10 years of homeschooling have helped me understand giftedness and gifted education in ways that continue to surprise me. In fact, because homeschooling parents learn with and from their children around the clock, homeschooling has much to teach all of us about what is real in education, what is truly important for gifted children and teens, and what parents can do at home to support their children's needs and dreams.

Like so many other parents, I first encountered the idea of giftedness when our son approached school age. When he visited our local public elementary school at age three, the gifted and talented coordinator suggested that he be screened for early entrance to kindergarten. My clearest memory of the part of the testing that I was present for is that at one point, he noted with delight that the flower in one of the sets of pictures was beautiful, and then he had to be reminded to answer the question. When the test results came in, the school's recommendation was that he would in fact be a good candidate for early kindergarten entrance. Because he was excited about the prospect, we agreed.

Despite his having begun public kindergarten a year early, by first grade, his teacher told us that our son already knew everything that she was planning to teach that year. She added that she wasn't planning to change a thing in her classroom to accommodate his learning needs. Additional challenge would come from a weekly, one-hour pull-out program with one other highly gifted student.

This was my first encounter with gifted programming. While the intentions of the school and the gifted and talented coordinator were good, the pull-out program was poorly planned and insufficient. Our son and the other student were often taken out of their normal classes in the middle of an activity and with no prior notice. The activities they did together seemed haphazard and not part of a larger plan, other than the school's being able to say that it provided gifted programming as early as first grade. However, these young gifted students were gifted all day every day, and not just the hour per week that they went to the pull-out program. The pull-out program was not likely to meet either their academic needs or their social needs; they needed changes in their regular classroom as well.

This was also the year when I became most aware of the emotional aspects of giftedness. Our son's combined introversion, sensitivity, and intensity made the activity and teasing of the playground, the din and smells of the cafeteria, and the bus ride home with third and fourth graders a daily challenge for him. He had begun kindergarten wide-eyed and eager to learn. Now he came home each day from first grade nearly in tears, and he was labeled "uptight" and, because he cried easily, emotionally immature.

Although I was on the school district's gifted and talented commit-tee, at mid-year, our family decided to switch to a very small private school for gifted children that specialized in early childhood education. There, I was highly involved as a parent and teacher. Our family learned much about giftedness during this time, and our son made some good friends who thought and felt as he did. When it was time to look for another school at the end of second grade, we decided to home-school—just for a year, just until we found a school that would be a good fit. Several other families from the school decided to try homeschooling at the same time, which provided a built-in support group for the parents and a peer group for our children.

At the end of each year of learning at home, our family reevaluated our decision, and each year we saw that homeschooling was working better than anything else we could imagine. Our son was back to his joyful self. He had time to explore his interests. He had a strong group of friends, both from the private school and from the local homeschooling community. He was enjoying learning in small, informal groups, and he had the right balance of time with others and time just with his family. Homeschooling also gave him the flexibility to learn at a level appropri-ate to his intellectual needs without formally skipping grades. It was during this time that I wrote *Creative Home Schooling: A Resource Guide for Smart Families* to share with others what we were learning and to pro-vide the information that I wished I'd had when we started.

Our "just one year of homeschooling" had turned into six, and before we knew it, we were at the high school crossroads. Family and friends began to say things like, "He'll be going to high school, right?" or, "What will you do now that you'll be finished homeschooling?"

For the first time, I was questioning our assumption that home-schooling would end after eighth grade. We had come to know many families whose children stayed home until college. Their teens were happy and well-adjusted and smart. They had a wide range of friends and broad interests. They got into good colleges. Most important, they weren't burned out from the typical high school schedule of early morning classes, after-school extracurricular activities, and hours of homework each night.

In the end, we left the decision up to our son, not at all sure what he would do. He requested information from private high schools and visited our local public high school before announcing that he was choosing to stay home. My first thought was "Good." My second was "Okay, now how do we do this?"

I gratefully picked the brains of other homeschool families about homeschooling for high school, and I found some good books on the topic. I learned that our decision to stay home for high school was not at all unusual and would not be as daunting as I had first thought. However, as I learned from others and we continued our homeschooling journey, I found myself—and heard many other parents of intense teenagers—still wanting and needing something more, something that addressed the unique needs of adolescents whose intellectual drive and emotional intensity fell outside the scope of most guidebooks, something that would reassure me that the questions we had and the challenges we faced were normal for who our child is, and that others shared our experiences. As our son grew older, not only did his needs change, but mine did as well. As a parent, I now had different questions, different challenges, and different moments of joy.

Faced with the need for something more and different, like any good homeschooler, I decided to do it myself—and write my own book. But, as often happens with books, what you have in your hands is not exactly what I had in mind when I started.

When I began to write what I thought would be the sequel to *Creative Home Schooling*, intended only for families who wanted to homeschool for high school, I not only drew on our own experience, but I also interviewed families of homeschooled teens, read everything I could find about homeschooling for high school, and delved into research about gifted adolescents. During this time, I also had the privilege of joining the board of directors for SENG (Supporting Emotional Needs of the Gifted), which strengthened my commitment to focus on the social-emotional aspects of giftedness and broadened my exposure to other parents and families with gifted teens.

Somewhere along the way, I realized that at least 90% of what I was writing wasn't about homeschooling specifically, but had more to do with living with and parenting intense, creative, and unusually bright teenagers, regardless of whether they learned at home or at school. While I will always be a strong proponent of homeschooling, I don't believe that it is the best choice for every family. I also realize that not every family who might want to homeschool can do so easily, due to particular family situations.

My research showed me that there are already some very good books in print about homeschooling during the teen years. There is also a wealth of information about young gifted children. What is needed is more information for parents about understanding and guiding gifted teenagers, homeschooled or not. So I began to focus my writing on what's different about gifted teens, especially their social-emotional needs and growth. This book is the result.

Parenting for an Extraordinary Kind of Success

A Parent's Guide to Gifted Teens is written from one parent to another, offering perspectives on intensity and giftedness and suggesting ways to make your home a good social-emotional fit for your family. I am not interested in the "parenting for future school and financial success" model of giftedness. This is not to say that many gifted adolescents don't have amazing success, both personal and public, or that such success isn't a good thing, but there is already plenty of advice for taking that path. This book has a different focus—the "emotional difference" articulated in this quote by the groundbreaking educator Annemarie Roeper:

> *Educators and experts in gifted education today see the gifted child in terms of what they do or are able to do and not who they are—not how their emotions differ from those of other children. They do not look at what motivates the child; they do not look at their Souls. In fact this word seems taboo in gifted child education. I believe and observe daily in my work that the gifted child has a complex Self that is driven by his other inner agenda. It is my belief that the gifted child is emotionally different from others.*[1]

Much of my understanding about giftedness is thanks to the writings and work of Annemarie Roeper, who co-founded The Roeper

School in Michigan in 1941 with her husband, George, modeling the school on the same idealistic beliefs and principles of the school they both attended in Germany before they were forced to flee from the Nazis. She writes that the traditional approach to education "defines human beings in terms of what they can do and how they can serve, not in terms of who they are."[2] She also warns of the dangers of educating "in isolated fragments" and educating "for the next step, the next test, the next grade, the next school."[3] For gifted teens in particular, the "next step" becomes ever higher and more stressful as time goes on.

Parents often feel enormous pressure to fulfill their children's potential, especially in adolescence when college and the world of work loom on the horizon. However, Annemarie Roeper believes that the role of the parent is not to fulfill the child's potential, but to offer guidance and opportunities that help the child know what will result in fulfillment:

> [P]arents see their task as helping their child fulfill his own destiny. Parents [should] open the door for the child rather than molding the child into a preconceived shape. To do this, parents must regard the child as an autonomous, self-contained entity, responsible for its own destiny. This allows the child's inner agenda to drive his learning.[4]

While many parents of gifted children feel a gut-level agreement with the above words, they are also frightened of actually implementing them or unsure of whether their teenagers can be trusted with responsibility for their own future. They might think that adolescents don't really know what's good for them and so must be prodded and poked to stay on the right track until they are mature enough to do so on their own.

The amazing potential of gifted teens can easily tempt parents and teachers to focus almost exclusively on making sure that such potential is not "wasted." Usually with good intentions, adults think of the middle school and high school years primarily as a time for young people to prepare themselves for college admissions, honors and awards, and lucrative or high-profile careers.

What can be lost in this process is what caused my husband and me to notice our child's giftedness in the first place. Think back to when you first realized that your children's intensity—intensity of learning, of emotions, of imagination—was different from the norm. Remember how their love of learning seemed to drive every question, every action, every waking moment. Remember the ways in which they challenged themselves just for the fun of it, the joy they took in novelty, and the learning that took place in the absence of standardized tests or grades or transcripts.

Now think of adults you know, whether young or old, who have maintained this joy of learning and who experience *Flow*—being in complete absorption—in their work and play.[5] Did they all follow the traditional "education for success" model in a smooth fashion? Did some of them have some missteps along the way or have years of what we might consider underachievement? Did they sometimes go against the advice of their peers or authority figures so as to follow their own voice, their own path? Was that path always the conventional one of high grades, good colleges, even better graduate schools, and six-figure salaries?

Adolescence is the bridge between those early years of wide-eyed wonder and what we hope will be a mature yet continual joy of self-discovery and exploration of the world. The self-consciousness of adolescence inevitably has an effect on teenagers' choices, moods, and behaviors, but the essential traits of giftedness do not go away. When we no longer see our older children take joy in their education and everyday life, we can ask ourselves what has changed and what we, as parents, can do to support and encourage our teens' natural intensity and love of learning.

Certainly some young people thrive in a rigorous college preparatory environment. They are internally driven to apply to the most competitive colleges or perhaps to start college earlier than classmates. Not all of these students are pushed by their parents or teachers. Many are following their passions and setting their own goals to please themselves rather than others, and they should be encouraged in their own personal dreams and decisions.

Many other teens, however, follow such a path reluctantly, either because they are given no choice or because they have internalized the message that a life without high societal achievement is a life failed. Still others choose not to play the game at all and are labeled "underachievers."

The problem is, as Karen Arnold found in her study of high school valedictorians, that academic success does not necessarily translate into career success or personal fulfillment. The time and focus necessary to be at the top of the class leaves little time for pondering questions of fulfillment or happiness and little room for focusing on an area of passion at the expense of the well-roundedness required for a perfect GPA. In short, as Arnold writes, school is often "the center of valedictorians' activities and identities."[6] She quotes one study subject 14 years after graduation:

Since high school, I had a general direction that I lived by, certain rules that all I had to do was do them: go to school, classes, do what they tell you to do. I did that well, I functioned well within that environment. But it didn't create much of an individuality or creativity within myself. I never really explored what I really wanted—what did I really want in life?[7]

In other words, what happens to high achievers when the vehicle for their success—school and its rules and structure—is no longer there? Will they be able to find within themselves their own rules and goals after they receive college acceptance letters? Will they discover their personal means of measuring success when they are no longer being graded? In the end, whether our children graduate at the top of their class or earn awards or public praise is less important than how they feel about their own potential, how well they understand themselves, and how confident they are in their ability to meet their own personal goals.

Home as a Good Fit: "Bringing Their Souls to Light"

One of the defining characteristics of gifted individuals is an inherent, intense, and seemingly unbounded love of learning. This drive to learn is what allows gifted children to soak up information quickly as toddlers, whether in the form of teaching themselves to read, grasping math concepts quickly, or internalizing the rules of physical games and activities so that they seem second nature. When the drive to learn is thwarted or curtailed, gifted students are denied a large part of what brings them fulfillment and happiness.

When the love of learning withers, parents can look to see what might not be working in the environment or if something else is troubling their child.

Of course, schools are important, and the choice and availability of high quality middle schools and high schools can make a tremendous difference in whether gifted teens thrive, merely survive, or struggle unnecessarily. In this book, however, I am less interested in what goes on in specific classrooms or schools than in what families can do in their homes. Often families have little choice of what schools are available or affordable, and while advocacy for improved programming is important, sometimes we also have to focus closer to home on whatever changes we can realistically effect. In addition, research suggests that passion for activities in gifted high school and college students is more related to things that happen outside of the classroom than to academic activities, and that lack of challenge at school, lack of enthusiasm on the part of some teachers, and peer pressure to "dumb down" all contribute to gifted students' lack of passion in the classroom.[8]

Rather than explore what can or should be available in the classroom for gifted teens, I want to explore how parents can make their homes the "good fit" that is so often talked about in gifted education, whether children learn full-time in a classroom or are homeschooled, or some combination of both. I also want to urge parents to remember that they continue to play an important role in their adolescents' growth and development. Parents need not give up on influencing their children in positive ways once adolescence begins—through the home environment they provide, the conversations they have, and the way they model adult choices, relationships, and behaviors.

Why do parent and teacher discussions of social-emotional needs of gifted individuals so often stop short at middle school or eighth grade? Do we assume that by the teenage years, the peer influence becomes too great to overcome? Or maybe the greater amount of time that teens spend away from home—at school, in extracurricular activities, with friends—seems insurmountable in terms of families having much of an influence on teens' growth and development? Is it because many teenagers seem to pull away from family as they work to establish their own identity, and parents sometimes disengage as well, unsure of whether they are wanted, much less needed?

Terri Apter, in *The Myth of Maturity*, reminds us that disengaging is the opposite of what our adolescent children need at this time:

> *Young people need their parents to focus on them in a way that brings their souls to light. Parents mirror growing children. They express pleasure or anxiety about what they do. A sense of self develops, good or bad, quick or slow, strong or weak, in tandem with a parent's responses. As children grow into teenagers and thresholders [young adults], they require a wide range of reflections that acknowledge the strangeness, the unexpectedness, the glamour of their growing self. However important friends and colleagues become, young adults still need from a parent the kind of eye-to-eye contact that says: "I see you, understand, and admire you."*[9]

Apter's eloquent words are a valuable counterweight to the idea of helicopter parenting. "Helicopter parent" is a pejorative term for parents who hover like a helicopter and are too involved in their older children's lives, ever watchful for problems that they can swoop in to fix and situations that they can control. These are parents who are not only inextricably involved in supporting and assisting their children's college application process, but choose the schools and co-write the essays. They call college deans to complain about grades. The dangerous lesson that they teach their children is that someone else will fix their problems and rescue them from failure, and the results are often that the young people feel helpless and do not develop resources for handling life's ordinary challenges.

While it is true that some parents are susceptible to micromanaging their children's decisions and lives (in Chapter 8, we will look specifically at how this temptation plays out in parents of gifted teens), the unfortunate consequence of the "helicopter parent" stigma is that some parents who have a normal and healthy level of involvement may worry inappropriately that they are over-involved.

Courageous Parenting

How can we be involved in our children's lives in a healthy way without crossing the line to helicopter parenting? Psychologist James Webb offers another alternative to the traditional "parenting for school and financial success" model—one that stresses creativity, courage, and caring:

> *We must try our best to give our children the knowledge to know the questions and the freedom to ask the questions, the caring to want to pursue the answers, the flexibility to create new answers when the old ones no longer work, the stamina to pursue the answers, the humanness to care about the outcome, and the courage to act with integrity.*
>
> *What I am proposing is idealistic, but I think that parents and educators of gifted children need to be idealistic. I hope that you will think more about creativity, courage, and caring—along with motivation and ability—but more so that you will be inspired to share your idealism with others.*[10]

Fostering creativity, courage, and caring in our children happens when we model those qualities in ourselves. Many difficult decisions about parenting gifted teens are made easier if we focus on these "three C's."

Creative parenting means you look beyond conventional wisdom to consider new approaches. You are creative when you allow your children to ponder several ideas, without judgment, before they finally make a decision. You are creative when you accept a certain amount of complexity and messiness in life as normal, rather than expecting quick fixes or only one solution for every problem.

Of course, parents care about their children, but practicing *caring* in a conscious way is something different. Caring is "having compassion, concern, or sympathetic interest in someone or something outside of ourselves."[11] We are caring when we listen to what our children are saying—*really* listen—without interrupting or prematurely offering advice. We are caring when we let our children know that we are concerned when they are concerned, even if we don't fully understand why they are troubled. We are caring when we work to see our children for who they are, apart from who we expect them to be.

Finally, you will need *courage* to stand up for your adolescent's needs, especially when they fly in the face of the expectations of others or traditional wisdom. You will need courage to support a teen who is afraid to voice or follow her ambitious dreams because she doesn't want to appear conceited in the eyes of her peers. You will need courage to support a young person's decision to choose a life of personal fulfillment rather than academic awards, although other adults are pressuring him to ignore his passions and instead follow a safer or more traveled path to success. You will certainly need courage to support young adults who have no idea what they want to do with their lives and feel undue pressure—either from within or without—to make life-changing decisions before they are ready.

How can we find and develop the best in ourselves—our own idealism—as we nurture our gifted children? To this end, I will sometimes ask you to think about some tough questions that will force you to look at yourself honestly in terms of your relationship with your child. This is certainly not because I want anyone to feel guilty or to imply that parents make a lot of mistakes. Parenting is on-the-job training at its purest, full of stops and starts and changes in direction to be sure, but I know that, as a parent who wants a deeper understanding of an intense teenager, you are ready for deeper self-understanding as well. Our own self-knowledge and wisdom reflect back to our children. As they see us continually improve and learn and live life more fully, our families and lives and community are all the richer for it.

Themes and Organization

A Parent's Guide to Gifted Teens is based on a few key aspects of giftedness:

- The unique *asynchrony*—or lack of fit—of gifted teens. This asynchrony may be more obvious in early childhood than in adolescence, as, for example, when a toddler who is not yet potty trained nonetheless teaches herself to read. However, asynchrony does not go away or "even out" in adolescence; it just looks different and requires a different understanding and accommodation.

- The unique *intensity* of gifted teens. This intensity occurs not only in the intellect, but also in the emotions, physical self, senses, and imagination. Understanding intensity will affect not only how you see your children's social and emotional growth, but your relationships within your family, and maybe even your understanding of yourself.

- The unique *precocity* of gifted teens. Highly gifted children may be ready for middle school or high school work long before they reach their teens. Similarly, they may show "symptoms" of adolescence—such as self-consciousness and a preoccupation with issues of identity—while still in grade school. Gifted students don't just work ahead; they often think differently from other students and benefit from different methods and resources, especially creative and self-directed approaches.

- The unique *parenting needs* for gifted teens. Let's face it: parenting an intense teenager brings with it challenges and questions that many other parents don't face or ask. At the same time, you may be relieved to know that much of what works for parenting gifted adolescents is the same good advice for all parents, just applied to different circumstances and somewhat individualized to meet your teen's (and perhaps your own!) intensity.

Each chapter that follows focuses on a specific aspect of giftedness as it affects the adolescent years: the vocabulary of giftedness, the intensity of gifted teens and the idea of excitabilities, social-emotional needs of the gifted, creativity and creative thinking, self-determination of gifted teens and how parents can encourage self-directed learning, multi-potentiality and how being "good at everything" affects finding a career, and gifted adults and how being gifted affects parents' relationships with their children. The final chapter concludes with some thoughts on worry, expectations, and forgiveness.

Throughout the book, you will find quotations from gifted youths on topics such as peer pressure, teachers and parents, alienation, creativity, grade skipping, and the gifted label. These quotations are from the book *On Being Gifted*, a collection of thoughts from 20 gifted high school juniors and seniors at a symposium sponsored by the American Association for Gifted Children.[12] The candor and insight shared by these teenagers are important reminders that gifted theory, research, and advice all have as their focus gifted individuals whose experiences cannot always be quantified neatly into a table or chart of results.

Each chapter except the final one ends with an annotated list of resources for further reading and research. My hope is that the pages that follow will be just the beginning as you give yourself permission to challenge traditional notions of giftedness and achievement.

I also urge you to allow yourself to find joy in parenting your intense teenager. There is a widely held myth that if children are having fun, they must not be learning. Similarly, many people believe that if parents are not stressed out and constantly complaining about their teenagers, they somehow are not normal parents or they are "too close" to their children or not "tough enough" with them. It's time to put those myths to rest and explore ways in which we can parent not only with creativity, courage, and caring, but with a joy that your children and you deserve.

Recommended Further Reading

The Myth of Maturity: What Teenagers Need from Parents to Become Adults
By Teri Apter
Norton, 2002
Teri Apter not only explains and debunks the myth of maturity, she also offers excellent insight into the workings of the adolescent mind, as well as how parents can learn to relate to the changing behaviors and needs of their teenage and young adult children.

Doing School: How We Are Creating a Generation of Stressed-Out, Materialistic, and Miseducated Students
By Denise Clark Pope
Yale University Press, 2004
While *Doing School* is not specifically about gifted adolescents, readers will immediately recognize the author's examples of fast-tracked, stressed-out students as intense and excitable. Pope's important book is a wake-up call to the dangers of ignoring children's and young adults' social-emotional needs for the sake of "a narrow definition of success."

The "I" of the Beholder: A Guided Journey to the Essence of a Child
By Annemarie Roeper
Great Potential Press, 2007
Annemarie Roeper's gem of a book is a powerful reminder to stay focused on the "Self" of the gifted child and teen.

Supporting Emotional Needs of the Gifted (SENG) Online Articles Library
www.sengifted.org/articles_index.shtml
The SENG website offers many well-written and useful articles on several aspects of giftedness, as well as free back issues of the *SENG Update* newsletter.

Chapter 2

Gifted, Talented, and Creative: What Does It All Mean?

What does it mean to be gifted? Or creative? Or talented? Is parenting a gifted child any different from parenting in general? Isn't everyone creative? Is extreme creativity an asset or a liability? Does talent need to be nurtured, or does it always rise to the top? Is the idea of giftedness elitist? Is giftedness a special learning need akin to dyslexia or ADHD? Does giftedness exist throughout the lifespan, or does it "go away" after early childhood? How does giftedness present itself in adolescents and young adults?

This chapter explores what it means to be gifted, talented, and creative, particularly for adolescents and young adults. If your child was identified as gifted at a young age, you will want to rethink how giftedness affects his life and needs now that he's older. Conversely, if you aren't sure whether your child fits the definition of gifted or talented, or if you don't know if her creativity is all that different from

> *People are prone to jump to conclusions about me solely because of any "gifted" image I may have; some people have already made up their minds about me or decided that I'm not their type. Some people don't think I could ever be interested in their more mundane things like parties or girls. (AAGC, 1978, p. 20)*

that of most other children, this chapter will help improve your understanding of her so that you can create a home environment that better accommodates her emotional and learning needs.

If, by the end of this chapter, you still aren't entirely sure if your child could be labeled "gifted" in a school setting, trust your instincts as a parent. What is interesting is that, at home, more important than using labels is providing an environment that nurtures sensitivity, encourages creativity, and supports individual interests and strengths. While being identified as gifted might be necessary for inclusion in school gifted programming—and for that reason very often worth pursuing—the gifted label itself is no guarantee of personal happiness or success, nor does it change who the learner is at the core of his or her self.

So, you might ask, why bother with definitions of giftedness at all, especially in the home? Why not just interact with every child according to individual needs, personality traits, and learning styles without using labels? One reason is that the experience of being gifted translates into being and feeling different, as the authors of *Talented Teenagers* explain:

> *Being talented means, by definition, to be different. There is no way to escape the implication of this fact. Most parents hope that their gifted children will grow up without problems and with many close friends, passing smoothly through adolescence into adulthood. But this very natural expectation is not very realistic.*[1]

Giftedness is a form of diversity that requires knowledge and understanding on the part of parents and teachers, especially because the messages from peers, the media, and society about giftedness often ignore the social-emotional needs of the gifted self, focusing instead on potential, academic achievement, and test scores.

Many gifted children, teenagers, and adults are painfully misunderstood by those around them. They are sometimes "put down" by parents, peers, and others for their sensitivity, intense emotional reactions, and strong opinions or views. Spoken or unspoken, the message tends to be, "Why can't you just be normal?"

Even more tragic, gifted individuals often fail to understand themselves and can spend their whole lives trying in vain to be "normal," especially if they receive the message, "I know that you are curious, talented, intense, etc., but can't you just be more like everyone else?" These individuals are keenly aware of their differences but believe that those differences mean that something is wrong with them. Rather than celebrate their uniqueness, they hide it in an effort to blend in with those around them. Their lack of self-worth can lead to denial of their abilities, feelings of being a fraud, or even serious, ongoing depression. Or they might become bitter and isolated, choosing to view everyone else as stupid or lazy. They often simply don't understand just how different from the norm they are or that most people just don't and can't think or feel as they do. When they learn that many of the traits that characterize them are common to gifted individuals, as well as that giftedness is one aspect of the great diversity of peoples in the world, they can better accept themselves and others.

Children's misconceptions about themselves are certainly influenced and compounded by the messages that they receive about themselves from others. Parents and teachers who do not understand giftedness are tempted to see a young child's high energy as a problem rather than a need for more or different stimulation. They might view a teenager's existential questioning as dangerous rather than a normal part of finding one's place in the world. And a college student's indecision with majors and career choices can look like flightiness rather than the expected struggle of someone who not only is interested in everything, but is good at it, too.

As parents, the better we understand giftedness, talent, and creativity—regardless of the labels we do or do not use—the better we can meet the needs of our children, and the more fulfilling our roles as parents can become.

Giftedness

If you are unsure of exactly what it means to be gifted, you are not alone. Questions about giftedness are not easy ones. There is no quick or simple litmus test for it. In fact, definitions of giftedness vary widely, are not always in agreement, and have changed several times over the years. Some definitions rely heavily on intelligence quotient (IQ) testing and set specific cut-off points for levels of giftedness; others do not include IQ scores at all. Some definitions include the idea of talents, grouping the "gifted and talented" together as one, while others draw a clear distinction between being gifted and being talented. Some theories propose that creativity is an inherent aspect of giftedness; some do not. Some definitions reserve the designation of gifted for only those who display motivation and accomplishment in areas considered valuable to society; other definitions maintain that giftedness can exist without any evidence of external achievement.[2]

Does this sound confusing? It can be, unless we keep our eye on what is really important.

The National Association of Gifted Children (NAGC) is considering the following definition of giftedness, developed by a task force of gifted education experts:

> *Gifted individuals are those who demonstrate outstanding levels of aptitude (defined as an exceptional ability to reason and learn) or competence (documented performance or achievement in top 10% or rarer) in one or more domains. Domains include any structured area of activity with its own symbol system (e.g., mathematics, music, language) and/or set of sensorimotor skills (e.g., painting, dance, sports).*
>
> *The development of ability or talent is a lifelong process. It can be evident in young children as exceptional performance on tests and/or other measures of ability or as a rapid rate of learning, compared to other students of the same age, or in actual achievement in a domain. As individuals progress through childhood to adolescence, however, achievement and high levels of motivation in the domain become the primary characteristics of their giftedness. Various factors can either enhance or inhibit the development and expression of abilities.*[3]

NAGC goes on to outline implications for educators, barriers to achievement, aspects of adult giftedness, and implications for policy makers.

The NAGC definition introduces four concepts at the heart of giftedness: achievement, potential, domains, and motivation. The first idea of achievement or competence refers to "documented performance or achievement in top 10% or rarer." When a child or an adult performs exceptionally or is a high achiever, we have no qualms in saying that the individual is gifted. For school-age children, documentation of performance or achievement usually has to do with grades, standardized test scores, and college admissions. However, for a variety of reasons (limited opportunities, test anxiety, or learning disabilities, for example), some gifted children may not test well; their "documented performance" is not a true measure of what they know or can do. NAGC recognizes that identifying giftedness in these students "will need to emphasize aptitude (potential) rather than relying only on demonstrated achievement."[4]

Third is the notion of domains—what we commonly think of as subjects of study, vocations, or focused interests. Because gifted learners are a diverse group, NAGC recommends that they "sometimes require additional and unusual learning interventions, not only of a general nature but also that increasingly target those domains in which they demonstrate the capacity for high levels of performance."[5] Providing learning interventions can be challenging when a child's area of interest is not valued or supported by society or when a child's focus falls outside of the usual elementary and high school curriculum.

Fourth, the definition recognizes the importance of motivation, noting that "As individuals progress through childhood to adolescence, ...achievement and high levels of motivation in the domain become the primary characteristics of their giftedness."[6]

Throughout this, the concept of aptitude or potential is inherent in our understanding of giftedness—specifically, the potential for extraordinary performance or high achievement. How do we best recognize or measure aptitude? Is the goal for potential always to be realized? Or is simply having high aptitude or potential enough?

Giftedness as Asynchronous Development

Asynchronous (out-of-sync) development is an important aspect of how giftedness is experienced. Asynchronous development simply means that a child's development is out of step with age peers, and also that levels of internal development are out of step with each other.

In 1991, a group of parents, teachers, and other advocates for gifted children—the Columbus Group—came up with the following definition of giftedness, which highlights the significance of asynchronous development in the gifted:

> Giftedness is "asynchronous development" in which advanced cognitive abilities and heightened intensity combine to create inner experiences and awareness that are qualitatively different from the norm. This asynchrony increases with higher intellectual capacity. The uniqueness of the gifted renders them particularly vulnerable and requires modifications in parenting, teaching, and counseling in order for them to develop optimally.[7]

This concept is easiest to understand in young gifted children because of their precociousness and rapid rate of development. Consider a gifted five-year-old who can do second-grade math and uses vocabulary three years beyond what is expected for his age. We might say that he has the mental age of an eight-year-old; his mental age and chronological age are out of sync. However, this isn't the whole story. At the same time, this kindergartener may have the small-motor skills of a preschool child, and he will likely be frustrated when he cannot spell the words that he thinks or neatly write the numbers that he can add in his head. His frustration is compounded by a higher-than-average emotional intensity and innate sense of perfectionism. All of this combines for a gifted difference that makes his inner and social experiences more complex than average, requiring specific understanding and accommodations from adults guiding his education.

When parents are aware of the areas of their child's asynchronous development, they can usually greatly minimize the child's internal and external struggles that result. For example, parents can take dictation for their daughter's stories until her motor skills are more developed. They can look for books and games that address and accommodate different levels of ability instead of learning resources that are created for a single age or grade level. Mixed-aged community groups and classes, such as book discussion groups that meet at libraries or chess clubs that meet at book stores, can provide gifted students with intellectual peers without the constraints of age-segregated classrooms.

Parents can also gently guide children toward management of what Mary Elaine Jacobsen, author of *The Gifted Adult*, calls an "urge to perfect"[8] by modeling a healthy acceptance of imperfections and mistakes, which is especially helpful for children with strong perfectionism issues. By allowing children to see adults make and accept mistakes, parents send the message that the pursuit of excellence is different from the impossible goal of constant perfection. Simple ways to do this include talking about your own past errors of judgment, as well as past successes; leaving less-than-perfect "in progress" writing or craft projects in view for children to see; and laughing off our human errors as sometimes inevitable, rather than berating ourselves in front of our children.

As gifted children move to middle school and high school, their asynchronous development can be less obvious to the untrained eye, but it is no less intense. For one thing, these children can experience the hyper-awareness of self and struggle with issues of identity—common to adolescence—long before they are teenagers. Their childlike bodies may still look like those of their nine- or 10-year-old classmates, but their minds and hearts are grappling with young adult questions of individuality, purpose, and belonging.

These children also can experience what can be described as an "idea-skill gap," meaning that they can envision doing things for which they lack the training or experience:

> *This idea-skill gap is extremely frustrating for the gifted students whose heads are like sparklers, firing off one idea after another. The frustration is compounded by the fact that many gifted young- sters actually excel at some things right off the bat, giving them the false impression that that is how it should be for everything they try. Consequently, they set the bar for everything accordingly, even those things that require years of training and effort.* [9]

For example, a gifted child who is taking violin lessons might hear in his mind (or on a recording) the "perfect" version of a piece that he is struggling to learn and come to the mistaken conclusion that his playing is "terrible" because his current version does not live up to the ideal. Or a young gymnast might reach a level of training that is suddenly much harder than before and be tempted to give up on her dream of compet- ing in the state tournament rather than put forth the extra effort to succeed at the new level. In these situations, parents can remind their children of times in their own lives when they needed to work harder or longer to reach their goals. We can tell them about of the hours of prac- tice required to learn a difficult musical piece or the hours of trial and error needed to learn new gymnastic moves—or to learn any new skill. Parents can also help children remember why they are doing the tedious work of practicing musical scales or stretching before every gym session. By keeping in mind what goal they want to accomplish and understand- ing the steps required to reach that goal, children can better withstand mundane tasks that lead to that end.

One might ask whether all children experience this frustration at some point. Of course they do, but for teens with unusually high levels of ability and sensitivity, the internal gap between what they want to do and what they are ready to do can trigger perfectionism, frustration, and despair. If they have no friends their age who share similar struggles, they also feel out of synch with their social environment. For instance, a high school student who is taking advanced calculus classes at a community college may tire of hearing jokes from friends about his being a nerd or geek and be tempted to settle for easier—if less rewarding—classes, especially if the college classes require more homework than he is used to. Without encouragement and support from adults or similarly gifted teens to follow his passions, regardless of peer pressure, he could assume that his drive to learn is too "weird" and deny himself the pleasure that comes from appropriate levels of challenge.

Does asynchronous development take care of itself as we get older? After all, we don't talk in terms of 20-year-olds functioning at a 30-year-old level, or a 40-year-old who doesn't fit in with age peers. Even when grade levels and the idea of mental age no longer apply, asynchronous development often continues to play a role in gifted adults' lives, especially if they have not found friends and colleagues who share their passion and intensity. Without self-knowledge and insight into the implications of uneven development, these adults can easily put all of their energies into honing their intellectual skills while allowing their social and emotional skills to atrophy, or they might sacrifice their intellectual abilities in an effort to fit in with the crowd around them. According to one psychologist who specializes in work with gifted adults, it is only when they reach a crisis point—often at middle age—that some gifted adults begin to know themselves for who they are.[10]

What Giftedness Looks Like

Because giftedness is so difficult to sum up in a neat, single-sentence definition, lists of traits and behaviors are often more useful as a way to recognize it. The following list is adapted from Annemarie Roeper's "Observable Characteristics of Gifted Children."[11] Annemarie Roeper was one of the first gifted education experts to stress the social-emotional needs of the gifted. How many of these traits and behaviors do you recognize in your children and/or other members of your family?

- Shows sensitivity
- Remembers insults forever
- Does three things at once
- Takes up lost causes
- Seems psychic
- Shows interest in death and life
- Is driven to understand; has complexity of understanding
- Wants to know the reasons for and origin of things
- Asks, "Why am I here?" and, "What am I to do?"
- Is naive, assuming that most others are idealistic, too
- Recognizes falsity; does not have "trophy friends"
- Prefers complex solutions to simple ones
- Finds non-conventional solutions; shows originality

- Is not motivated by extrinsic awards; feels discomfort with praise
- Is passionate
- Is undeterred by conventional expectations
- Teaches oneself
- Enjoys non-sequential learning
- Has a need for precision
- Recognizes unfairness to self and others
- Has a strong sense of justice
- Makes intuitional leaps and logical projections
- Notices what no one else notices
- Manipulates and bargains
- Makes and follows one's own plans
- Is not always teachable
- Devises practical experiments to see "What if?"
- Says "actually," wanting to be precise
- Has a large vocabulary and a love of big words
- May be delayed in toilet training
- Has difficulty in separating from mom
- Has an early sense of responsibility
- Does not want to grow up and face the world
- Avoids physical risk-taking
- Zips through Piagetian developmental stages[12]
- Has friends of both genders
- Shows later sexual interests than age peers
- Is an abstract thinker before having the emotional ability to handle it
- Thinks symbolically
- Can animate fears, such as "seeing" monsters in the corner of the bedroom, resulting in a very real upset stomach
- Possesses a powerful emotional imagination

The above list isn't a test. There is no cut-off score that indicates if someone is gifted or not, nor a range of points that will tell us that someone is "a little" gifted, moderately gifted, or highly gifted. However, if you see your child (or yourself) in many of the above descriptions, you can be assured that knowing more about giftedness will be helpful for your family. Also, please keep in mind that, because giftedness is complex, some gifted children may exhibit traits opposite to those described. For example, instead of being delayed in toilet training, a gifted child might teach himself to use the bathroom at an unusually early age (as our child did), or instead of showing a later-than-usual sexual interest in peers, a gifted teen may have sexual feelings long before most of her age peers. In other words, the goal isn't to be able to check off every characteristic, since no gifted child will fit that particular profile.

Is Giftedness an Elitist Idea?

Some people complain that the very idea of giftedness is elitist, that all children are gifted, or that gifted education gives resources and attention to the very children who need it least. After all, gifted children will do just fine on their own, right?

More than once, when I've spoken about giftedness at conferences, parents have told me that they felt they had to sneak into the session, fearful of what their friends would think of them. What is interesting is that these parents do not attend the session because they want to brag about their children or because they want to be in "elite" company with other parents of children considered gifted and talented. They come because they are confused and concerned. Pretending that their children are like most other children just isn't working any more. They need something different from the usual parenting information.

If we're honest with ourselves, we'll admit that our gifted children aren't the only ones who must deal with peer pressure. Many parents are competitive (sometimes without realizing it), easily envious, and most likely confused and worried that their children will be okay and find their way in the world. They also probably don't understand that giftedness is an internal difference that our children can't control and that can be as challenging as it is welcomed.

Parenting is not a job for wimps, and parenting a gifted child is even less so. We must resist the temptation to convince ourselves that our children's differences are always problems to be fixed, or that by providing for our children's emotional and educational needs, we are being elitist or egotistical. We don't need to wear a "My Child Is Gifted" t-shirt, but we can learn to listen to what is really behind the criticisms of those who don't understand. When I hear someone say, "Everyone is gifted," what I hear is, "I believe that everyone is special by virtue of being human," or, "Everyone deserves to think of himself or herself as unique and important." I couldn't agree more. I also believe that everyone has talents, many of which are unseen and untapped, and everyone has creative potential. However, that's not the same as everyone's being gifted. Giftedness is a combination of higher-than-ordinary ability, asynchronous development, and unusual intensity and drive that is not common to everyone. And whatever anyone else says, working to understand giftedness and meet the intellectual and social-emotional needs of our gifted young people is the right thing to do for them and for society.

I also have a sneaking suspicion that the most vehement critics of the word "gifted" and of the concepts of giftedness and gifted education are perhaps, themselves, misunderstood gifted adults.

Levels of Giftedness

Some children don't have just higher-than-ordinary ability, they have abilities either in specific subjects or globally that are "off the charts," far beyond what adults expect or what classrooms usually accommodate, such as being able to manipulate numbers in their heads in a way that the vast majority of adults can never do. Some children's development is so asynchronous that finding friends and intellectual peers seems nearly impossible, as when a five-year-old is reading books meant for middle school students but is not yet fully toilet trained, and thus has difficulty attending kindergarten. And the level of intensity and drive in some children is not only unusual, it also is almost overwhelming; they insist on doing things their own way, regardless of the consequences, and may refuse to cooperate with the expectations of adults.

Deborah Ruf, in her book *5 Levels of Gifted: School Issues and Educational Options* (formerly titled *Losing Our Minds: Gifted Children Left Behind*), distinguishes between five levels of giftedness, from what is generally known as "moderately gifted" (the top one-third to one-fourth of most classroom students) to "exceptionally" or "profoundly gifted" (ranking in the 99th percentile and higher on standardized tests and having IQ scores of 141 and above—roughly a handful of persons per million in the population).[13] Profoundly gifted young children will often teach themselves to read by the time they enter preschool and spend nearly all of their waking hours asking questions and soaking up new knowledge with an intensity that is both amazing and exhausting.

In short, gifted children are not all the same, and their needs can differ considerably. For example, while a moderately gifted high school freshman may thrive on AP (Advanced Placement) classes and find friends by associating with upperclassmen, a more highly gifted teen may need to do college-level work and will find much in common and to talk about with graduate students and adults. Exceptionally and profoundly gifted children may be ready and eager to delve into high school course work before middle school age. Such students often progress rapidly through high school-level curriculum and complete at least some of their secondary education by age 15 or even younger. Many parents of these children find that homeschooling is the best way to accommodate their adolescents' extremely asynchronous development, since homeschooling can allow many profoundly gifted children to learn at a pace appropriate to them, without restrictions of age, grade, or lags in motor skills or social-emotional development.

If you think that your child's giftedness falls outside of the usual description of gifted traits and behaviors, do some Internet research and visit your library to learn more about highly and profoundly gifted children, starting with Dr. Ruf's *5 Levels of Gifted* and Hoagies' Gifted Education site's "Highly, Exceptionally, and Profoundly Gifted" Web page (www.hoagiesgifted.org/highly_gifted.htm).

Talking to Teens about Giftedness

Many parents are uncomfortable talking to their children and teens about giftedness, afraid that such discussions might lead to arrogance or egotism. In some cases, parents even discount teachers' suggestions that a child might be gifted and instead insist that all ability and achievement are the result of hard work alone. At the other extreme are parents who seem to find a way to drop the word "gifted" into every conversation about their child.

> *Probably the only single thing all twenty of us agreed on back in New York—in all our lives— was that we hate the word "gifted." It's flattering, it's pleasing, but it alienates us from friends.* (AAGC, 1978, p. 4)

Regardless of whether you emphasize the word "gifted" with your children, it is important for intense, bright teens to understand that the differences they experience are not only real, but valuable. Of course, being born with a higher-than-average ability and drive to learn does not make one a better person. It does, however, often make one feel at odds with most of the world, especially in the age-segregated world of middle school and high school.

When our son was middle school age, we addressed the topic of giftedness in these ways, which have also worked well for other families:

- We used the ideas of intensity and excitability (which we will learn more about in Chapter 3), rather than focusing on the word "gifted." The idea of giftedness was too vague for him to relate to, whereas he could readily see that he was intense and excitable.

- We acknowledged and discussed the fact that his curiosity, emotions, and imagination were very strong, and that other people didn't necessarily share those traits. Even his friends who were gifted did not have the same excitabilities. Some were more physically excitable, for example, or more imaginative.

- We encouraged him to seek friends who shared or respected his differences. For example, with one friend who shared a strong imagination but who otherwise had different passion areas, he played complex games of make believe. These games began as outdoor spy games when the children were younger and grew to complex "what if?" and philosophy discussions in their teen years.

- We also tried our best to model for him a respect for the differences of others, including respecting the fact that not everyone is born with an intense, excitable nature. While it is extremely valuable for gifted youth to find intellectual peers, my experience is that their friendships certainly need not be limited by others' intellectual ability, especially if we encourage our children to learn to seek and value the differences in others.

- Finally, it is important for teens to know that being gifted does not automatically make one successful. We all—regardless of our abilities—need skills of organization and old-fashioned hard work to get things done. In fact, parents should probably not praise their children for being smart or gifted. As we'll learn in the next section, such praise leads to the mindset that one's ability is fixed and can also lead to perfectionistic thinking.

Talent

What is the difference between giftedness and talent? The authors of *Talented Teenagers: The Roots of Success and Failure,* offer this description of talent:

> *Talent is a social construction: It is a label of approval we place on traits that have a positive value in a particular context in which we live. In some cultures, epilepsy is considered a divine gift; in others, people who are overweight are admired. In our culture—one increasingly dependent on the manipulation of symbolic information—intellectual skills, especially those that tend toward logic and quantification, are considered valuable talents.*[14]

In other words, while giftedness can be thought of as an inner intensity, asynchronous development, and a unique experience and awareness of the world—all of which happen inside ourselves—talent, while also originating from inside, is usually thought of as an outward manifestation of potential in a specific area. Whether and how much talent is recognized is based largely on what society deems useful and important.

The terms "gifted" and "talented" are often used interchangeably or together in a phrase, as in "gifted and talented youth." Can a person be both gifted and talented? When someone is described as being talented, what the speaker or writer often means is that the person is gifted, or perhaps talented in many areas. However, being talented in and of itself begs the question, "Talented in what?" For our purposes, being gifted refers to a combination of high ability, asynchronous development, and inner drive and intensity; and having a talent refers to high potential—the ability to do better than most other people—in a specific activity or area of study.

For example, a child might have a talent for playing the piano. She learns quickly, has unusual mastery and dexterity of her fingers on the keyboard, and plays with poise and feeling, as well as technical control. Whether anyone—including herself—knows about her talent, however, depends on many things: whether she ever has access to a piano, takes lessons, has a mentor who encourages her, sets aside the time to practice, has the motivation and interest to learn, and so on. The talent can lie dormant or be used. Giftedness, on the other hand, is not used or developed as much as it is *experienced*.

Talents can also be in specific aspects of an activity. One can have more of a talent for composing music than performing it, for example, or a talent for the technical aspects of piano playing and sight reading, required for professional accompanists, rather than interpretative playing. Ken Robinson, author of *The Element: How Finding Your Passion Changes Everything*, writes about how finding our *Element*—or the fit between what we are good at (our talents) and what we are passionate about—is worthy of a lifetime quest and can lead to great personal joy and fulfillment.[15]

Talents—especially unusual talents, many talents, or high levels of talent—are often indicators of giftedness.[16] If you know that your child is talented but haven't before considered whether he or she might be gifted, review the list of gifted characteristics on pages 24-25. Learning more about giftedness might help you in raising your talented child.

Talent Myths

Talent development is an important part of education. Recognizing, valuing, and nurturing talent helps young people find their place in the world and can lead to not only personal joy, but better medicine and science, works of artistic beauty, great performances, and social improvement. However, the idea of talent is also clouded by two common myths.

> *Having multiple talents (I use the word loosely) allows you to dabble into a lot of different things. Consequently, you learn a little about a lot of things— which I think is important in order that you develop a broad spectrum of diverse interest, and in the process, meet hundreds of very interesting people.* (AAGC, 1978, p. 6)

Myth #1: Talent takes care of itself. Many people think that having a talent in a specific area means that one doesn't need to work hard or doesn't need as much individual attention and help as less talented peers. For example, a talented young writer who can whip off grade-A papers the night before a deadline certainly wouldn't benefit from individual attention. Or would he?

Some children never learn what they are truly capable of in a talent area because they aren't challenged sufficiently or they don't have someone to show them how to learn higher skills. Malcolm Gladwell writes in *Outliers: The Story of Success* that, "Achievement is talent plus preparation."[17] Gladwell argues that the kind of achievement that can bring us personal fulfillment is as much about opportunity, preparation, and continued motivation as it is about innate talent. He cites research by K. Anders Ericsson suggesting that expertise among musicians, and others, requires 10,000 hours, or roughly 10 years of practice. Gladwell concludes, "The people at the top don't work just harder, or even much harder than everyone else. They work much, much harder."[18] Think about the motivation and excitement about learning that is necessary for any person to devote 10,000 hours to an activity!

In addition to *Outliers*, another good resource to help parents understand the important role of self-efficacy and effort in success is psychologist Carol Dweck's book *Mindset: The New Psychology of Success*. Dweck describes the "fixed mindset" that exists when we believe that our abilities are set, innate, and unchanging. People with a fixed mindset have a "single goal of proving themselves—in the classroom, in their careers, and in their relationships. Every situation calls for a confirmation of their intelligence, personality, or character."[19] The fixed mindset leads to fear and even avoidance of effort because effort becomes a sign of deficiency. The growth mindset, on the other hand, "is based on the belief that your basic abilities are things you can cultivate through your efforts."[20] In the growth mindset, effort is a sign of growth rather than inadequacy.

Consider our talented writer. Without continued excitement to learn and proper encouragement and guidance, he might grow up thinking that his talent means that he doesn't have to practice as hard as other people. He doesn't need to work to learn writing skills because he has been told that he already has them—the fixed mindset. He might get less personal attention in honing his writing because teachers focus on the students who need help—whose talents lie in areas other than writing. The result is that our student's talent is never developed to the point at which he can make a living writing in a competitive marketplace, much less fulfill his own dreams of being a published poet or novelist or playwright. The first time he receives harsh criticism on a written assignment, perhaps in college, he might convince himself that he was never talented to begin with, and his motivation will rapidly diminish.

However, if our student is given the opportunity to be challenged sufficiently so that he needs to work hard to do well, and if he puts in the time necessary to write every day, just as a talented pianist would practice every day, he has the chance to use his talent for himself and others.

Adults can also be careful not to discount a child's talent or take it for granted. A musical family, for example, may not see anything extraordinary about a child's teaching herself to play the piano, since such behavior and ability is the norm within their experience. When others repeatedly point out a child's talent in a particular area—especially if it is a talent that you as the parent have not noticed or paid much attention to—refrain from assuming that others are just being "nice," and ask yourself if you might be missing an area of passion or talent in your child that you could better support.

Myth #2: Talent should not be wasted. What does it mean to waste talent? Do people who have a clear talent area have an obligation to society to develop that talent and to use it in their careers? Do they have an obligation to themselves? In 1993, the U.S. Department of Education went even further, arguing that "America's talent" must be developed so that we as a country can "compete on equal footing with the rest of the world."[21]

What could be wrong with that perspective on talent? The problem is that talent development and excellence, when understood in this way, are by definition measured in terms of academic or performance success. If talented students are doing well in school, or in sports or music or art, then we must be meeting their needs. Similarly, if they are not at the top of their class or team, they somehow are not fulfilling their potential. The idea of talent development as an obligation can very quickly turn into neglect of the inner experience of being gifted, as well as dismissal of the role that passion plays in both personal fulfillment and success.

Ken Robinson, mentioned previously, believes that we do often neglect our true talents because either those talents aren't valued by or they fall outside of traditional education.[22] A boy with a talent for drawing, for example, might never see where this talent leads him if his more valued talent for math and physics means that he is dissuaded by adults from taking art in favor of AP science and math classes. After all, being a working artist is not what our society values in terms of being on an "equal footing with the rest of the world." Or a girl with a talent for math could easily miss the joy of higher mathematics (and many varied career choices, such as engineer, statistician, economist, or medical researcher) if she is convinced by a school aptitude test or school counselor—against her instincts and passions—that she should become a preschool teacher.

Robinson argues that instead of looking only to traditional academic areas for signs of talent, as measured by grades and standardized tests, we look for those areas where our aptitudes or talents meet our passions—our *Element*. We might very well have talents in areas that simply don't interest us. This is especially true for those gifted teens who are good at many things. What is the main talent area for a student who has a 4.0 GPA, plays first chair violin, is on two varsity sports teams, and is student council president? Rather than focus on finding his greatest talent area, he might be better served by asking himself what is his greatest passion area. If he buys into the myth that any talent not developed is a talent wasted, he will inevitably be torn and feel guilty, because whatever he chooses, some of his talent areas will be "wasted" more than others. Or he will be spread too thin, trying to develop multiple talent areas.

Some people don't discover their talents or the passion for their talents until later in life. Some explore their various talents serially, moving from one to another. Others pursue their areas of passion and talent as hobbies rather than as a way to make a living. In such cases, can we really say that early talent was wasted because it was not funneled into a lucrative career?

Rather than have the goal of developing our children's talents, we can instead work to help them explore their talent areas and discover which ones they truly enjoy and want to pursue further. This process is far from easy and contains many false starts, decisions, and struggles, but as the authors of *Talented Teenagers* remind us, "No teenager will develop talent unless he or she enjoys working in the talent area."[23] The role of self-motivation is essential. For this reason, as James Webb often says in his talks to parents of gifted children, when your child shows interest in and talent for music, rent the piano or clarinet instead of buying it, until you know that the passion and motivation are lasting. Malcolm Gladwell puts it this way: "Talent is the desire to practice.... It is that you love something so much that you are willing to make an enormous sacrifice and an enormous commitment to that, whatever it is—task, game, sport, what have you."[24]

Talking to Teens about Talent

- Don't be afraid to acknowledge that your child may have talents in specific areas that allow her to pick up skills faster than others. Pretending that natural, innate talent does not exist does not help children to know themselves and may lead to the fixed mindset that Carol Dweck describes. For example, if a young gymnast doesn't realize that she is naturally more flexible than her teammates, she might think that such "success" comes without work, unaware that real success is what she does to build on her natural ability. Instead of praising her natural ability, we can say, "That comes easily to you. It's probably time to try something harder."[25]

- Avoid sending the message that "talent is enough." Talent is a starting point, a gift. What we do with our talents is what we can own and can bring us satisfaction. For example, when we watch a musical theater production that features accomplished singers, we can say, "How much work they must have spent to master those musical numbers!" instead of, "What talented singers!"

- Encourage children's interests, regardless of whether or not they show talent in that area. In *The Element*, Ken Robinson quotes Paul McCartney, who says that when he and George Harrison were in school, "no one ever thought we had any musical talent at all." McCartney was rejected by the Liverpool Cathedral choir, just as Elvis Presley was told by the glee club that his voice would "ruin their sound." Similarly, comedian John Cleese of Monty Python fame says that he showed academic talent when he was young, but all the way through college, no one noticed in him a talent for humor.[26] If, as Gladwell, says, talent is indeed "the desire to practice," then practice and motivation may be more telling than early recognition of natural ability.

- For perfectionistic gifted children in particular, we can watch for any interests they have that fall outside of their areas of strength or talent because these interests provide valuable practice in working hard toward personal goals. Suppose your usually non-athletic daughter says she wants to learn to figure skate. You hesitate to encourage her because you know that she is not particularly well-coordinated, you realize that she is older than the average beginning skater, and you wonder whether the practice and lesson time would cut into her studies. However, if she is truly interested in getting on the ice, the ups and downs (literally) of learning to skate forward and backward, spin, and maybe even jump offer valuable experience in not only diligence, but also in living with imperfection. Figure skating coaches say that skaters fall hundreds of times before they land their first jump. There is no shortcut, and no one gets it right the first time.

- As a family, read or listen to the audio version of Malcolm Gladwell's book *Outliers* or Ken Robinson's *The Element*, both of which are appropriate reading for interested teens who want to understand the roles of work and motivation in the successful use of talent. Then, together, discuss the authors' examples and theories. Talk about your own talents, both those you use on a regular basis and those that you have not developed as much as you could.

Creativity

Just as with the word "talented," the word "creative" is often paired with "gifted." Similarly, creativity is not exactly the same as giftedness and is often misunderstood.

Perhaps the simplest explanation of creativity comes from Jane Piirto, author of *Understanding Creativity*, who writes that creativity is "a basic human instinct to make that which is new."[27] Using this definition, creativity is common to all of us, just as we all have talents of varying strengths and in different areas.

One aspect of creativity is divergent thinking—a way of thinking that generates many different ideas and possible solutions. Divergent thinkers prefer "the unusual, original, and creative aspects of any topic."[28] Think of

Robert Frost's poem in which "Two roads diverged in a yellow wood." Suddenly, instead of the one expected path, we are presented with choice and complexity. People who prefer divergent thinking embellish rather than stick to the script, get off track rather than stay on task, and are easily bored by activities that box them into a corner.

Convergent thinkers, on the other hand, rather than being drawn to the unusual or seeking many ideas or possibilities, direct their thinking toward the expected or "the one right answer." They enjoy activities that allow them to ignore rather than seek extraneous possibilities. They are often very good at memorizing facts and figures, and they may be uncomfortable with tasks that are open-ended or subjective. Rather than look for diverging paths, they are good at finding their way back to the main road.

Think about your family's dinner table conversations. What kinds of questions do you ask? Are they mostly convergent questions that point to one, discrete answer, such as, "What grade did you get on your history test?" or are they divergent questions that encourage open-ended thinking, such as, "What are some new ideas for how we can spend our summer vacation?" When you talk about your day or discuss current events, do you usually assume that there is one correct way that things should be (convergent thinking), or do you try to see and present situations and people from different or unfamiliar points of view (divergent thinking)? Begin to pay attention to your own patterns of thinking and how they might differ from, hinder, or support those of your children.

Neither divergent nor convergent thinking is superior in general, although for specific tasks, one might serve us better than the other. Stand up comedians who improvise, for example, need to be able to think divergently "on their feet" and come up with several different, even competing ideas at once. Accountants, on the other hand, cannot afford to indulge in divergent thinking as they prepare individual or corporate tax returns, at least not without legal ramifications. That said, learning to think in both ways is a valuable skill in almost any field. Convergent thinkers can practice divergent thinking in order to find answers that they would otherwise miss, and, as one writer on creativity reminds us, "divergent thinking is not much use without the ability to tell a good idea from a bad one."[29]

Although divergent thinking is just as valuable as convergent thinking, children who are strongly divergent are at a disadvantage in the traditional classroom, especially on standardized tests, where convergent thinking—generating the one correct response—is what is valued. Psychologist Deirdre Lovecky explains, "Many children who are divergent thinkers appear to be disorganized and absent-minded, particularly in school. While adults can compensate for their absent-mindedness by choosing life styles that reward divergent thinking, it is more difficult for children."[30]

What Creativity Looks Like

Divergent thinking is only one aspect of creativity. Creativity is by its very nature complex. In fact, as we'll learn in Chapter 5, having a complex personality is a necessary component of personal creativity.[31] Because of its complexity, creativity (just as with giftedness), is often easier to recognize than explain. Common traits of highly creative people include that they:[32]

- Are sensitive
- Are not motivated by money
- Are intuitive
- Are observant
- Ask questions
- Have a strong sense of humor
- Are curious
- Tolerate ambiguity
- Can be very critical
- Are self-disciplined
- Are energetic

You might want to spend some time thinking about this list. Do any of the items surprise you? In Chapter 5, we will learn more about the role of self-discipline and critical thinking in creativity.

Giftedness and Creativity

How does creativity fit with giftedness? The answer, as you might expect, is complex. Many definitions of giftedness presume a high degree of creativity. For example, Ellen Winner, author of *Gifted Children: Myths and Realities*, writes that gifted children are by nature creative,[33] and Joe Renzulli's three-ring Venn diagram model of giftedness includes these three overlapping traits: above-average ability, task commitment, and creativity. Other writers suggest that while high intelligence is necessary for creativity, it is also true that one can be extremely intelligent without being highly creative.[34]

What we probably can agree on is that, just as unusual talent can be an indicator of giftedness, so can unusual creativity. This is an important consideration for parents and teachers because highly creative children are often overlooked for inclusion in gifted programs and may even be seen as disruptive in the class. A highly creative child may challenge the teacher, have another way to solve a problem, or want to modify the writing assignment. Because it can disrupt their lesson plans, teachers sometimes don't like or appreciate this kind of gifted child.

Think again of the traits of creativity listed above. If a school system bases its criteria for giftedness on convergent traits (being able to do well on standardized tests and provide expected answers, for example), it's easy to see how a creative child—one who considers alternative answers, displays extreme curiosity at inopportune moments, or questions the authority of teachers and other adults—would not easily fit into the gifted model.

Regardless of what happens in the classroom, parents can play a crucial role in helping a highly creative child use his creativity in his education and life rather than stifle it and, more important, to understand his own creativity as valuable and wonderful rather than problematic. For many, if not most, highly creative children and adults, giftedness—and the intensity of giftedness in particular, which we turn to in the next chapter—is an important part of who they are. Understanding giftedness is important in helping creative children thrive.

Talking to Teens about Creativity

- Just as with giftedness and talent, it is good to acknowledge, but not praise, a child's creativity. Understanding that some people are more creative than others—more divergent in their thinking, more drawn to new and unusual ideas, more tolerant of opposing views, better able to synthesize different topics and ideas—not only helps creative children to understand themselves, it also helps them to see that others don't necessarily think the way they do.

- Talk about how family members differ in their preference for creative thinking. One easy way to begin discussing this is with a home activity like cooking. Do you always follow a recipe, clean up as you go, and get anxious if you don't have the "right" ingredient? Or do you find recipes restrictive, prefer to make up dishes based on available ingredients, remain unbothered by a pile of dirty dishes, and get excited by having to make new substitutions for missing ingredients? A simple family discussion of these differences can throw light on the value of both kinds of thinking.

- Provide highly creative teens with plenty of outlets for their creative and divergent impulses. Especially if they are in a rigorous college prep program, most of their day is probably spent doing tasks and thinking in ways that go against their creative grain. At home, do what you can to relax strict timetables and encourage flexibility, and talk with your teens about ways to do so. This might mean cutting back on evening activities to allow for more free time for the entire family.

- Encourage your children to build "improv time" into their activities and studies. Our son's piano teacher, for example, tells his students to build into their practice time a period of improvisation, when they make up their own songs just for the fun of it. In addition to assigned homework, encourage your teens to make time for free reading and writing for the fun of it.

- Refrain from limiting how they think of themselves by saying things like, "Rosa is hopelessly disorganized. After all, she's the creative type." Also, don't make the mistake of thinking that creative learners cannot learn convergent thinking skills in order to gain the knowledge base necessary for achievement and success. If your teen shows a creative talent for art, for example, she will benefit not only from drawing what she wants, when she wants, but also from learning art history, studying art techniques, and honing the ability to practice on a regular basis. Such skills may not come naturally for the highly creative, but they are not out of reach. Look for organizational approaches geared to creative strengths. Two good resources are *Dreamers, Discoverers & Dynamos: How to Help the Child Who Is Bright, Bored and Having Problems in School* (formerly titled *The Edison Trait*), by Lucy Jo Palladino, and *Organizing from the Right Side of the Brain: A Creative Approach to Getting Organized*, by Lee Silber.

- If a teen's strong creativity is causing conflicts with a teacher or getting in the way of completing school assignments, discuss with your adolescent the roles of convergent and divergent thinking, and encourage him to talk to the teacher about his frustrations.

He might even think of ways to negotiate with his teachers for more creative thinking in the classroom and with his homework, such as proposing an original essay topic rather than the assigned topic—one that still fulfills the purpose of the assignment but that allows him to branch into a divergent direction. Or, if a teacher complains of his constant questioning, he might ask if he could lead a discussion session on a particular controversy or write an opposing viewpoint to what is being learned in class as a way to satisfy both his creative impulse and the teacher's need to cover specific topics.

Recommended Further Reading

Growing Up Gifted: Developing the Potential of Children at Home and at School
By Barbara Clark
Prentice Hall, 7th edition, 2008
This gifted education textbook is also a valuable resource for parents who want a comprehensive understanding of all of the aspects of growing up gifted, including social-emotional development.

And Still We Rise: The Trials and Triumphs of Twelve Inner-City High School Students
By Miles Corwin
William Morrow, 2000
Miles Corwin follows the senior year of 12 gifted students in a South-Central Los Angeles inner city high school, where "the peer pressure to fail is oppressive." Often using the students' own words, Corwin tells the stories of the obstacles they face and what it takes for them to rise from their circumstances.

Talented Teenagers: The Roots of Success and Failure
By Mihaly Csikszentmihalyi, Kevin Rathunde, & Sam Whalen
Cambridge University Press, 1993
This fascinating study of Flow and talent in adolescence also offers specific guidance for how parents can create a nurturing and challenging home environment.

Mindset: The New Psychology of Success
By Carol Dweck
Ballantine Books, 2007
Psychologist Carol Dweck describes in detail the difference between the "fixed mindset" and the "growth mindset" and discusses how parenting practices help shape how and whether children feel in control of their own growth and success. Parents can learn more about Dweck's theory and work at her website: http://mindsetonline.com.

Outliers: The Story of Success
By Malcolm Gladwell
Little, Brown & Company, 2008
Written by the author of *The Tipping Point* and *Blink*, *Outliers* is a thought-provoking discussion of some of the patterns of success, including the role of hard work and sustained effort.

The Element: How Finding Your Passion Changes Everything
By Ken Robinson
Penguin, 2009
Ken Robinson's inspiring book about finding the meeting place between what we are good at and what we love—our *Element*—draws on examples and stories from Paul McCartney to Matt Groening, Arianna Huffington to Richard Feynman. The book was born of the lecture "How Schools Kill Creativity," available online at www.ted.com/talks/lang/eng/ken_robinson_says_schools_kill_creativity.html.

A Parent's Guide to Gifted Children
By James T. Webb, Janet L. Gore, Edward R. Amend, & Arlene R. DeVries
Great Potential Press, 2007
If you could buy only one book about giftedness in children, this would be it. Some of the many topics covered include characteristics of giftedness, communication, discipline and self-management, perfectionism, and friends.

Hoagies' Gifted Education Page
www.hoagiesgifted.org
You can spend hours browsing articles and links on this "all things gifted" Web page.

Chapter 3

The Intense Teen

In the third episode of the documentary *The National Parks: America's Best Idea*, writer and producer Dayton Duncan describes his feelings as he watched lava flow from the Kilauea Volcano at Hawaii's Volcanoes National Park:

> *[Y]ou were watching new land. For an Iowan, new land is a great notion. I felt like I was in the earth's maternity ward. You know that euphoric rush you get if you walk into a maternity ward and see all those little babies? Well, here was a little bit of land being made where that lava met the sea.*[1]

Duncan's words and work are a powerful example of intensity—intensity of intellect (knowledge of the volcanic process), intensity of emotions (the euphoric rush he feels), intensity of the senses (seeing and describing the details of the lava as it meets the sea), and intensity of the imagination (the metaphor of new land as new life). In addition, Duncan's intensity of personal energy allows him to do the work necessary to turn his idea into reality. He says of his work:

> *I have the best job in America. I don't even consider it a job. My "job" is to pick a topic that I'm interested in, convince Ken [Burns] that we ought to do a film on it, and then begin with what I call sort of a self-directed, post-graduate degree in that topic.... I had to spend a number of years reading about the individual parks and reading about the history of the park idea. The second part of it is then to find the people who know the most about the topic and meet them and talk to them. Then we would interview them, going out on location.*[2]

The intensity that Duncan describes and exhibits is the driving force behind not only memorable works of art, but also the "euphoric rush" of otherwise ordinary life.

The Difference of Intensity

Understanding intensity is invaluable in understanding gifted children and gifted adults, as well as helping them to understand themselves so that they can lead fulfilling lives. While we tolerate and even appreciate intensity in adults, especially when it leads to work or art that we value, we often misunderstand, discourage, or even punish manifestations of that same intensity in young people.

The editors of the ground-breaking book *Living with Intensity: Understanding the Sensitivity, Excitability, and Emotional Development of Gifted Children, Adolescents, and Adults* explain intensity this way:

> *[Living with intensity] means that life is experienced in a manner that is deeper, more vivid, and more acutely sensed. This does not just mean that one experiences more curiosity, sensory enjoyment, imagination, and emotion, but also that the experience is of a different kind, having a more complex and more richly textured quality.*[3]

In other words, the experience of people who are highly intense is truly different from that of many other people. They live at a faster or more reflective internal pace, seek knowledge and answers as though their lives depend on it, or exude an energy that leaves those around them exhausted. They are usually quite idealistic and often strive passionately to reach their ideals, sometimes showing perfectionism.

I love to talk and I need to talk. When the appropriate companion is not present and efforts to converse with the person waiting for the bus are futile and de-energizing, I feel like running away. (AAGC, 1978, p. 11)

This difference of intensity is a type of diversity that can cause gifted teens to compare themselves unfavorably to more mellow, less intense peers, leading to the mistaken conclusion that something must be wrong with them. However, this difference—their intensity—can also lead to great joy, satisfaction, and personal growth, particularly if young people understand and learn how to work with their intensities rather than be ashamed or overwhelmed by them.

Overexcitabilities

One way to understand intensity is through the theory and work of Kazimierz Dabrowski, a Polish psychiatrist, psychologist, and researcher. Dabrowski studied areas of intensity—the word he used is usually translated as "overexcitability"—common to people with potential for personal and emotional growth. Michael Piechowski, who has written extensively on Dabrowski's theory, says that the closest English word for what Dabrowski meant is "superstimulatability." In his book *"Mellow Out," They Say. If I Only Could: Intensities and Sensitivities of the Young and Bright*, Piechowski uses the terms "heightened excitability" and "aliveness."[4]

Some people try to avoid using the word "overexcitability" because "over" can connote negative excess. However, for our purposes here, I will use either "overexcitabilities" (because this is the term most recognized by experts in giftedness at the current time) or "excitability," keeping in mind that such excitability is quite different from hyperactivity or simple nervousness.

The authors of the award-winning book *A Parent's Guide to Gifted Children* explain the difference posed by overexcitabilities:

> [G]ifted children are particularly prone to experience these over-excitabilities. The idea is that gifted children's passion and intensity lead them to be so reactive that their feelings and experiences far exceed what one would typically expect. It can be compared to the difference between receiving information with rabbit-eared antennae versus a satellite dish. These children either experience or respond to stimuli in a much more intense way.[5]

Dabrowski focused on five different areas of excitability that contribute to overall intensity. The following descriptions of the overexcitabilities are adapted from Piechowski.[6]

Intellectual Overexcitability

What it means:
- ○ Intensified activity of the mind
- ○ Passion for probing questions and problem solving
- ○ Reflective thought

How it shows itself:

- ○ Curiosity, concentration, capacity for sustained intellectual effort, avid reading, keen observation, detailed visual recall, detailed planning

- ○ Search for truth and understanding, forming new concepts, tenacity in problem solving

- ○ Thinking about thinking, love of theory and analysis, preoccupation with logic, moral thinking, introspection (but without self-judgment), being able to integrate intellectual concepts and intuition, independence of thought (sometimes very critical)

Emotional Overexcitability

What it means:
- ○ Feelings and emotions intensified
- ○ Strong physical reactions to emotions
- ○ Strong emotional expressions
- ○ Capacity for strong attachments, deep relationships
- ○ Clear and well-understood feelings regarding oneself

How it shows itself:

- ○ Positive feelings, negative feelings, extremes of emotion, complex emotions and feelings, identification with others' feelings, awareness of a whole range of feelings

- ○ Tense stomach, sinking heart, blushing, flushing, pounding heart, sweaty palms

- ○ Inhibition (timidity, shyness), enthusiasm, ecstasy, euphoria, pride, strong emotional memory, shame, feelings of unreality, fears and anxieties, feelings of guilt, concern with death, depressive and suicidal moods

○ Strong emotional ties and attachments to persons, living things, places; attachments to animals; difficulty adjusting to new environments; compassion; responsiveness to others; sensitivity in relationships; loneliness

○ Inner dialogue and self-judgment

Imaginational Overexcitability

What it means:
○ Free play of the imagination
○ Capacity for living in a world of fantasy
○ Spontaneous imagery as an expression of emotional tension
○ Low tolerance of boredom

How it shows itself:

○ Frequent use of image and metaphor, facility for invention and fantasy, facility for detailed visualization, poetic and dramatic perception, animistic and magical thinking

○ Predilection for magic and fairy tales, creation of private worlds, imaginary companions, dramatization

○ Animistic imagery, mixing truth and fiction, elaborate dreams, illusions

○ Need for novelty and variety

Psychomotor Overexcitability

What it means:
○ Surplus of energy
○ Physical expression of emotional tension

How it shows itself:

○ Rapid speech, marked excitation, intense physical activity (e.g., fast games and sports), pressure for action (e.g., organizing), marked competitiveness

○ Compulsive talking and chattering, impulsive actions, nervous habits (tics, nail biting), workaholism, acting out

Sensual Overexcitability

What it means:
- ○ Enhanced sensory and aesthetic pleasure
- ○ Sensual expression of emotional tension

How it shows itself:

- ○ Intensified seeing, smelling, tasting, touching, hearing; delight in beautiful objects, sounds of words, music, form, color, balance

- ○ Overeating, sexual overindulgence, buying sprees, wanting to be in the limelight

Intensity and Personal Growth

Each of the five areas of excitability can be frustrating and painful, especially for teenagers who are already easily embarrassed and don't like being pegged as different. However, Dabrowski proposed that over-excitabilities, rather than necessarily being negative traits, play a significant role in helping people to develop their human potential—to grow from who we are to who we want to be.

This growth is a process that, according to Dabrowski, involves not only idealism—to see how things might be—but also disappointment and "positive disintegration." Disintegration happens because we are dissatisfied with some aspect(s) of ourselves, our life, or our interaction with the world in which we live—something that happens particularly frequently in bright adolescents and young adults. This disintegration, though often accompanied by anxiety and depression, can be positive; we can use our dissatisfaction to move beyond where we now are to become something more, such as more giving, more understanding, more disciplined, more skilled and knowledgeable, or more resourceful.

Disintegration is seldom a one-time event. It's not a matter of disintegrating, coming out whole and "fixed," and never being dissatisfied again. Disintegration can occur several times in one's life as a person grows in awareness and maturity; it can also be a cyclical process in which a person is dissatisfied, experiences some negativity—whether a relatively minor depression or state of anxiety or a larger crisis at adolescence or midlife—and then gradually moves on to a new and better understanding, a more positive outlook, or improved emotional health. The five areas of overexcitability—especially emotional and intellectual excitabilities—impel us toward self-reflection and personal problem solving as a way to develop our personal potential.

People with overexcitabilities can be highly sensitive and react intensely to both their inner and the outer worlds. Intellectual over-excitability leads them to "ponder and question," emotional over-excitability "makes them more sensitive to issues of morality and fairness," and imaginational overexcitability prompts them "to envision how things might be." One can see that, while overexcitabilities can bring richness and depth to life, they can also trigger the existential awareness and depression that we see in so many gifted adolescents and adults, particularly those who are more highly gifted.[7]

Therefore, it is important that people who experience overexcit-abilities not just learn to tolerate them, but seek to understand them, to see them as positive, and to work to manage them. The anxiety or dis-comfort caused by overexcitabilities is not in itself positive. Instead, the benefit comes from "the individual's consequent self examination and emerging insight into day-to-day life and a deeper, more conscious and multilevel understanding of his or her reactions."[8]

In our lifetime, we might experience several periods when we seem to take two steps (or more!) back before leaping forward, but adoles-cence is one of the most common triggers for the kind of disintegration that, for people with intensity, has the potential to be a transformative or tragic experience:

> *Adolescence, rife with disintegrative experience in all spheres of knowing, is a time of great expectancy. In fact, adolescents can be terror ridden with the awareness of the possibilities of what could be or the feeling of the inevitability of what will be. In optimal circumstances, though, a disintegrative experience can be a trium-phant transcendence of a young person's way of being.*[9]

Think about your own teenage years and those of your siblings or friends. Was it a time when you questioned the values of your teachers and parents while also feeling doubt or guilt for doing so? Did you simultaneously feel that you were in a chrysalis stage, struggling to slip out of an outgrown shell but not yet ready to expose new, fragile wings to the air? Were you torn between feelings of grandeur and limitless potential on the one hand and tormenting self-doubt on the other?

Finally, when did you begin to come out of your disintegration, and what positive value met you on the other side? Was it the result of insight gained through difficult self-examination and reevaluation? Was it the support and understanding of key adults around you? Was it experiencing difficulties and self-doubt until you gradually gained confidence in yourself? Did you then find yourself moving toward another round of dissatisfaction and potential development? As an adult, have you had times when you questioned your values or decisions or purpose in life? Did you change your circumstances or behaviors as a result? This is the kind of growth that Dabrowski wrote about.

The theory of positive disintegration is much richer and more complex than this brief overview. If you are curious to learn more, see the list of resources at the end of this chapter. For our purposes here, what is important is that having high levels of intensity can be seen as not just good, but also as extremely valuable, especially when we take the long view of lifespan learning and growth.

The rest of this chapter looks at each area of excitability in more detail, especially in terms of adolescence, and offers suggestions on how to help teens (and ourselves) work with, rather than against, our intensities. You might recognize your child (and yourself) in one or two areas of overexcitability, or in all five.

Intellectual Excitability

Consider two students in a biology class. One studies diligently and learns the terms easily. He aces the tests but never really engages with the material and doesn't think about the subject except in the context of getting a good grade on his transcript to help his GPA and college applications later. When he closes the book in his hands, the subject is closed in his mind as well. Another student studies the same material but finds herself fascinated by the subject matter. She looks up more information than is necessary and continues to think about what she learned long after she hands in the test.

The first student is book smart. The second student is intellectually intense. One college student I know describes the intellectual intensity of "being into a lot of things":

> *My own learning style is very independent and stubborn, in a way. I need to do things in my own way and on my own terms. I have a hard time understanding something like a process or how to*

do something from instructions alone or from seeing someone else do it. I need to try to do it and to figure out how it works on my own. Also, I can remember times when I memorized what I needed to in order to pass a class but retained almost nothing. Then I went back to the text later when the class was finished and actually learned the material. I really have to be into something for it to stick with me. Luckily, I'm into a lot of things—art, veganism and animal rights, literature, and all areas of science, particularly ecology and genetics. I spend much of my free time playing the piano, studying Classical Greek, reading, and making delicious vegan desserts.[10]

Intellectual excitability is not the same as just being smart or academically successful. High achievers certainly can have intellectual excitability, and many do, but they might not, just as students with intellectual excitability might not necessarily do well in school.

What differentiates intellectual excitability from intellectual achievement is an internal drive to learn and to use one's mind to explore and interact with the world and with oneself. When paired with good study skills and a desire to get good grades, intellectual excitability *can* lead to extraordinary academic success. However, some intellectually overexcitable young people simply don't care much about whether they get straight A's, or they may not have developed the self-discipline and organizational skills to give evidence in a classroom of just how much they know. In fact, research suggests that some gifted adolescents may lag behind their age peers in skills of executive processing, such as long-term planning and decision-making[11] (see Chapter 6). In addition, some students may have a strong intellectual curiosity and a "rage to master" and learn in areas that are not traditional academic areas.[12] Thus, external academic achievement is not a reliable indicator of intellectual excitability.

Intellectual excitability is easy to recognize in young children because they have fewer barriers to their natural passions and drives. For example, a four-year-old who is teaching herself to read usually has the time, resources, and encouragement from adults to continue to learn. A seven-year-old whose passion for nature is not satisfied in the classroom might obtain the information he needs by asking questions, going to nature centers with his parents, or watching nature shows and documentaries.

By the time these children are teenagers, however, they may find that their once-insatiable drive to learn is now thwarted by a day full of non-challenging classes, hours of homework, after-school and weekend sports and other activities, and perhaps chronic fatigue from lack of sleep. On the outside, our once precocious readers and nature lovers may seem to have lost their intellectual intensity. On the inside, they just can't find the time or energy to pursue what once made them so happy.

Here are some indications that teens might have intellectual excitability, regardless of their level of academic achievement:

- They use language well and are aware of how well others do (or do not) use language.

- They may be impatient with others who do not learn as quickly or remember as well as they do.

- They are easily bored when they have already mastered a topic.

- They notice and remember details that other miss.

- They use free time to play complex games (whether on or off the computer).

- They enjoy conversation with adults who share their interests.

- They read nonfiction books or magazines that are written for adults or professionals.

- They are keenly interested in issues of truth and justice and may be idealists.

- They are the masters of debate and argument, never tiring of finding new ways to present their opinion or side of a case.

Some teens with intellectual excitability get frustrated with others who don't think as quickly, deeply, or precisely as they do. This is one reason that gifted children benefit from knowing and learning with intellectual peers. When they are in the company of someone else who can keep up with their train of thought, share their joy of complex games and problem solving, and challenge their ideas, they are less likely to assume that "no one" understands them.

For example, in his latter years of high school, our son showed a strong interest in the 2008 presidential election, an interest that developed into a passion for political history and public policy. He spent many hours happily reading blogs, current interest magazines, economics textbooks, and political biographies. However, he was also sometimes frustrated by two parents who, while having a passing interest in such topics, do not share his intensity in these areas, nor, at this point, his knowledge base. Not until he got to college and took his first classes in political science, history, and economics did he find professors and students with whom he could discuss these issues at his level of interest. In such cases, it is important to encourage young people to continue their interests and not to stop looking for kindred minds—whether through advanced classes, mentors, programs for gifted youth, or in appropriate online forums.

When intellectually overexcitable teenagers learn and live in environments that accept and support their intellectual needs, the results can be extraordinary. These teens will still experience the angst and disintegration of adolescence, but they will also explore areas of their own minds and hearts otherwise hidden, pushing themselves to the edge of their capabilities in order to see just how far and wide they can go. In doing so, they

> *I used to and still do spend hours in book stores, pacing and picking. I have yet to be able to walk into a book store without any particular literature in mind, browse for a few minutes, decide on a book and purchase it. Packing and picking—I wore out the floor trying to decide. The problem is, I want them all. I want to read and discuss, and discuss and read. For what good is knowledge if it is not shared to make another person happy?* (AAGC, 1978, p. 11)

learn a valuable truth—that they needn't fear nor hide their drive to learn.

Emotional Excitability

People who are emotionally overexcitable can seem at times to be ruled by their emotions. How they feel is tied up with everything they do: how they learn, how they relate to other people, how they think about themselves. It's not just that they feel *more* than other people; they also feel *differently*, in the sense that their emotions are closer to the surface for them and are more integrated with their experiences. Their emotions can also be an important source of self-knowledge and can provide clues to understanding others.

Young children with emotional excitability may cry often, be easily embarrassed, be attuned to the feelings of others at an unusually young age, and form strong attachments, not only to family members, but also to pets and even inanimate objects. As they mature, they usually learn to manage their emotions to a certain extent, but the excitability is still there and can rush forth at full throttle in adolescence. The usual emotional roller coaster of the teenage years is an even wilder ride when combined with the trait of emotional excitability.

> *Somehow I knew, once you had experienced the deepest possible state of sadness, maybe over the death of your dog, the exact same feeling would prevail over the death of your mother. Though the causes differ, the reactions were limited in their degree of expression. I knew this early in the short time I'd lived and it silenced me.* (AAGC, 1978, p. 18)

This doesn't mean that all teens with overexcitable emotions wear their hearts on their sleeves. Peer pressure and acute self-consciousness can cause young people to bury their feelings deep inside, afraid of being out of control and wary of their own intensity. Especially if they have no one with whom to share their feelings and if they feel that their intense emotions are a sign of weirdness or being somehow "broken," emotionally overexcitable teens can easily suffer from depression and despair.

Here are some manifestations of emotional excitability in teenagers:

- Their memories are based on feelings as much as factual details.

- They feel a responsibility for others or take up causes, even to the point of self-sacrifice.

- They are shy or self-conscious.

- They have a tendency toward depression.

- They value peaceful relations and interpersonal harmony.

- They are self-reflective regarding their actions and emotions.

- They worry about issues of life and death more than other teens.

- They seem to absorb the emotions of people around them and may have trouble setting personal boundaries or separating their own feelings and needs from those of others.

- Their self-talk can sometimes be based on false assumptions, leading to incorrect conclusions about self and others.

- They may have a strong mind-body connection that causes them to feel physically ill when they think about or witness certain acts or scenes or when they are under great stress, especially if they also have a strong imagination. Illness can be anything from stomach upset and nausea to more serious "gut" issues, nervousness, muscle tension, or other complaints.

Some of the best ways that parents can support emotionally excitable teens is by accepting their excitability and helping them take control of their feelings by making good choices for themselves. Some emotionally excitable teens, for instance, realize on their own that they need to be more careful than their friends in what kinds of movies they watch or video games they play. They have learned that violence—whether physical or psychological—is not good for their emotional health. One college student I know adjusts the settings on video games when he can to minimize the on-screen depiction of blood and gore, and another avoids watching or listening to the news before doing homework because she knows that she may hear something that will make her too upset to concentrate. The important thing is that we encourage children to make these decisions because of how they want to feel—as a way to take care of themselves, and not because anything is wrong with them or because they are "too sensitive."

Parents of emotionally excitable teens can find themselves the target of their child's excitability. If you are on the receiving end of adolescent tantrums, door slamming, or hurtful speech such as, "I hate you and can't wait to leave this family!" know that you can learn how to respond in ways that lessen the toll on yourself and that discharge some of the emotional intensity. Two excellent books that offer practical suggestions for how parents can talk to and improve relationships with their teenagers are *How to Talk so Teens Will Listen and Listen so Teens Will Talk*, by Adele Faber and Elaine Mazlish, and *Stop the Screaming: How to Turn Angry Conflict with Your Child into Positive Communication*, by Carl Pickhardt.

In short, emotional excitability can be painful. Emotional teens might not understand why they have to feel everything to the extent that they do or why others don't seem to feel much at all in comparison. Especially before they reach full emotional maturity, they have a hard time managing their feelings or being able to pause long enough to think about them objectively. The value of emotional excitability, however, is great. It can be the source of great compassion, lifelong loyalty, appreciation of beauty and goodness, and aesthetic production. When adolescents can learn about the gifts that their emotions offer, they may be better able to tolerate the more difficult moments.

Imaginational Excitability

Imaginational excitability in young children is evident in their fantasy play and the ease with which they slip between real and imagined worlds. We expect and value a strong imagination in young children. As children grow older, however, we too often expect them to put away childish things, including their wonderful sense of imagination. If we do allow for imaginative thought, we confine it to art class or theater and discourage it in the more "serious" subjects of math and science.

Albert Einstein reminded us, "Imagination is more important than knowledge. For while knowledge defines all we currently know and understand, imagination points to all we might yet discover and create." It's hard to think of a career that doesn't benefit in some way from a little daydreaming and imagination, if only to help us to do our work better through visualization. In fact, imaginative and creative thinking are useful in everyday problem solving, from figuring out how best to rearrange room furniture to deciding how to revise the family budget so as to afford college costs or an overseas vacation.

In schools, however, imaginative thinking often is not encouraged, and students who have imaginational excitability may either deny this part of themselves as they plod through test-driven curriculum or be labeled "scatterbrained" or "distracted."

Teenagers probably no longer have (or admit to) imaginary playmates, but they show imaginational excitability in some of these ways:

- They often use metaphors when they speak or write.
- They enjoy fantasy-based computer or role-playing games.
- They often seem lost in worlds of their own making.
- They like to invent things: stories, solutions, tools, or art works.
- They choose fantasy reading or movies.
- They write poetry or stories for their own enjoyment.
- They remember their dreams and nightmares in vivid detail.
- They imagine (and perhaps fear) the future and the unknown.

Because many adults seem frightened by the power of children's imaginations, imaginational excitability is often not supported in the same way as intellectual excitability. Michael Piechowski writes that "down-to-earth people" see an excitable imagination as "an ominous departure from reality" and that children with imaginational excitability are easily dismissed, especially those "creative youngsters born into task-oriented, reality-bound families."[13]

Adults should be careful not to dismiss imaginative play as childish. We can never know what imaginative power might lead to in the future. One girl I know spent nearly a year as a preschooler pretending to be a dog, much to the discomfort of adults, who expressed concern to her mother that something was wrong with the child. Her mother's patience and wisdom paid off, however. Eventually the girl's strong imagination found other outlets, her interest in animals never waned, and as a high school student, she worked as an apprentice to a dog breeder.

Jane Piirto, in *Understanding Creativity*, recommends that parents enhance creativity by allowing "their child to be 'odd'" and by not "emphasizing socialization at the expense of creative expression."[14] She writes of noted film-maker Steven Spielberg, who used his childhood experience of imagining a creature that lived behind the wall of his bedroom to create the character of E.T. Similarly, Leo Tolstoy, creator of the rich worlds of *Anna Karenina* and *War and Peace*, spent hours as a child with his brothers, huddled under tents made with chairs and cloth, imagining their own secret world in which misfortune did not exist.[15]

When teenagers understand and own their imaginative excitability, they have access to powers of visualization, dreams of a better society, empathy with nature, fantasy, and creative expression.[16] An active imagination is also an almost instant cure for boredom.

Psychomotor Excitability

Psychomotor excitability, or what Piechowski calls "personal energy," can be easier to recognize in young children than in teenagers. A young child with psychomotor intensity is impossible to miss! She's the one who never naps, who doesn't walk when she can run or skip, and who doesn't sit when she can stand or dance or do gymnastic stunts. She might wiggle and make faces while thinking or watching television, or she may need to use her hands in order to pay attention when being read to aloud. She talks quickly and seemingly non-stop.

By the time this young girl reaches adolescence, however, a host of changes can mask her psychomotor intensity. Hormone changes and lack of sleep may leave her tired and listless. Years of training to sit still at a desk may have taught her to control her impulse to move while she thinks, except for the occasional rhythmic foot movement or finger tapping. While the urge to speak quickly is still inside her, the fear of what others might think and the pressure to fit in keeps her thoughts silent.

Psychomotor excitability is not the same as having athletic talent (although the two are not mutually exclusive). In other words, while a star basketball player might have psychomotor excitability that enhances and drives his practice and performance, he might just have natural athletic ability, just as a student with psychomotor intensity who is always on the go might lack physical coordination or athletic skills. Many children with psychomotor excitability prefer individual sports, such as swimming, running, or martial arts, over team sports.

Do any of the following indications of psychomotor excitability remind you of young people you know?

- They like to be involved in many activities and don't like to "do nothing."

- They complain about situations in which they have to stay still for long periods of time, such as car rides or long lecture classes.

- They have nervous habits or tics, such as nail biting or hair twisting.

- They like to keep their world organized and spend energy keeping their room and space to their liking.

- When allowed to do so, they move around as they learn or do homework, switching chairs or positions or moving from room to room.

- They are physically impulsive, often moving before they think.

- Their psychomotor intensity might be expressed more strongly when their emotions run high, such as pacing the room when they are stressed about studying for standardized tests or needing more physical release of energy when they are worried about an illness in the family.

Teenagers who have boatloads of personal energy are at risk for overextending themselves, sacrificing sleep and health habits in order to fit in just one more activity, one more hour of study. However, if psychomotor excitability doesn't seem like much of an asset, think of adults you know who get a lot done. You know the ones—they never complain about being busy but nevertheless accomplish more in a day than most people do in a month. They might have jobs that keep them on their feet for most of the day. Although others may see them as already overcommitted, they readily say "yes" to most requests and, rather than regretting their response, relish the opportunity to try something new. They are involved in many different activities with family, co-workers, friends, and volunteer groups. Not everyone has the energy for such a life. Psychomotor excitability is what makes it possible.

Sensual Excitability

Sensual excitability is an area of intensity that many people overlook as a positive and instead see as problematic or irrelevant. We can think of it as heightened and pervasive sensations, especially the five physical senses of taste, touch, smell, hearing, and sight. Infants who are sensually overexcitable might cry when put in non-cotton sleepers, or they might finger a favorite soft blanket until it is threadbare. As they enter school, these children can find themselves distracted by the sound of florescent lights buzzing overhead or another student tapping a pencil on the desk. They are often highly attuned to food tastes and textures, finding foods such as cooked tomatoes or mushrooms slimy to the point of initiating a gag reflex. They also are easily overstimulated by sights, smells, and movement. The competing strong smells, bustle, and chatter of a school cafeteria can make them so tense that they are unable to eat.

Just as with emotional excitability, sensual excitability is easily repressed in teens who are fearful of what others might think of them. This is especially true for boys in a culture that stereotypes sensory astuteness and appreciation as a possible sign of homosexuality.

Teens of both genders can show excitability of the senses in these ways:

- They appreciate comfort in ways that others their age do not, preferring soft or natural fibers in their clothes, specific colors in their room décor, a near-silent work environment or one with very specific background sounds, or certain weather conditions or indoor temperatures.

- They notice and appreciate beauty, whether in the natural world, artwork, literature, music, or everyday scenery and objects.

- They might hear or be distracted by noises that others don't notice, to the point of being unable to concentrate if, for instance, a clock is ticking in another room.

- They can be very sensitive to tastes and smells and may enjoy fine food, cooking, and dining.

- They might have a low tolerance for feeling dirty.

- They might be extremely bothered by specific flavors and aromas, limiting their choice of foods or use of scents.

- They might enjoy being the center of attention, whether in informal groups or on stage.

- They may seek stimulation in various ways, which may include thrill seeking or sensual activities.

- They like to feel good and may have a narrower range than others of what conditions allow them to feel good.

In an effort to feel good, teenagers who are sensually overexcitable may overindulge in eating, shopping, drinking, sex, or other addictive behaviors. Learning how to use one's sensual excitability for self-nurture without being self-destructive is an important skill for them to master. For some people, intense exercise or sports—such as running, martial arts, or swimming—offer sensual pleasure that satisfies their excitability in a health way. Other teens might enjoy fabric or needle arts such as sewing or knitting, playing musical instruments, handling and caring for pets at home or as a shelter volunteer, or practicing visual arts such as oil painting, charcoal drawing, or pottery.

Having sensual excitability can also lead to great appreciation of beauty. People with sensual excitability can use their senses for joy and pleasure in ways that many other people cannot even dream of. For adults, the ability to lose oneself in an art museum or at a symphony is preferable to turning to medications or alcohol for stress relief. When teenagers learn to understand and use their own senses to bring themselves joy and comfort, they learn a valuable life-skill that goes far beyond high school and college.

Sensual and other excitabilities also affect a teen's experience of sexual development. Stephanie Tolan, award-winning author of young adult and children's fiction and a popular speaker on the topic of exceptionally gifted children, describes the roles of intensity and asynchronous development in gifted adolescence:

> *Their bodies work from a normal clock—the hormones come into play according to the children's physiological maturity; their minds*

work from a different clock—the cognitive consideration of sexual issues usually begins early; their feelings work from still another and, according to Dabrowski, with unusual intensity.[17]

In other words, while the body clock—the hormonal and physical changes of puberty—might be more or less "on time" for gifted teens as compared with other children, their experience of puberty can be complicated by an earlier-than-usual intellectual understanding of what is happening to them and a more intense emotional reaction. Also, keep in mind that, as with all children, some gifted children will naturally experience the physical aspect of puberty earlier or later than average. In all cases, the psychological and physical changes are accompanied by both advanced intellectual abilities and unusual intensities. Here are just a few examples of what asynchrony can look like during the process of sexual maturation and understanding:

- A pre-adolescent boy might show few outward signs of puberty but nevertheless be driven to educate himself on all aspects of sexual reproduction, sexually transmitted diseases, and gender issues. Even if parents restrict online information by filtering Web content, precocious and intellectually driven children can find much information the old-fashioned way—by looking it up in books. Parents in this situation may be unsure of how to address their child's seemingly "too early" interest in such matters, or they might worry that knowledge will lead to unwanted behaviors and experimentation.

- A gifted child might show very early physical signs of puberty while lacking the executive functioning and judgment skills necessary to make wise decisions and, at the same time, experiencing emotional excitability that heightens sexual feelings. These children can easily mistake others' attention to their physical maturation as affection or respect. Especially if a young person feels unconnected to peers or family and that she is misunderstood, she can be tempted to latch on to sexual behavior in lieu of friendship or as a way to satisfy intense sensual overexcitability. Or, for young girls in particular, early physical development can lead them to withdraw into themselves to avoid unwanted attention.

- Some gifted children go through puberty later than their age peers, adding to a sense of being different and out of sync. While classmates are dating and beginning to look like adults, they feel trapped in a child's body. If their intellectual abilities are unusually high, they might feel that they are even more of an oddity. The extreme self-consciousness of the teen years combined with introversion or emotional intensity can make it very hard for such children to take the first step toward showing romantic interest in boys or girls they like. Or gifted teens might show a later interest in romance and dating simply because they are focused on and getting satisfaction from their education and other pursuits, and they know that having a relationship at this time in their life—with all of its teenage drama—will get in the way of their passions and goals.[18] One of Annemarie Roeper's observable traits of gifted children is that they often show later sexual interests than age peers.[19]

In all of these cases, the gifted difference has an effect on parenting. Parents should be careful not to compare their children's needs or changes with those of friends and classmates, or even to other gifted children. They can let their children know their expectations for sexual conduct. They can also anticipate that they might need to discuss issues of sexuality earlier than they had expected, and they need to be ready for conversations when children begin to ask questions. Annette Revel Sheely, counselor and teacher at a school for the gifted and creative, reminds us, "Research has shown that giving young people honest information about sex does not promote early sexual activity."[20]

Sheely's article "Sex and the Highly Gifted Adolescent," available on Douglas Eby's Talent Development Resources website,[21] is a clear and valuable resource for guiding gifted teens toward a healthy sexuality. Sheely advises that parents be open to whatever their child wants to discuss in terms of sexual feelings or behavior. While it can be tempting to try to force personal information from adolescents, such coercion is not as effective as working to create a safe space for open dialogue and questions. Parents can begin by sharing their own stories of what they felt as teenagers, especially moments of awkwardness or uncertainty.

Parents who are unsure of how to broach the subject of sexuality can use television and movies as a way both to talk about specific situations, such as teen pregnancy, sexual orientation, or abusive relationships, and to communicate their own expectations and beliefs. For example, after watching a movie about teen pregnancy, you might ask your teenager for her thoughts about what happened on the screen as a way to gain insight into her developing attitudes and knowledge. If, in the course of such a conversation, a son or daughter shares information that the parent finds uncomfortable—such as sexual experimentation or homosexual feelings—parents can be careful not to overreact, which can close the door to future communication. Instead, adults can accept the information as an indication of trust and allow some breathing and reflection time to pass before making any big decisions or judgments.

Parents who expect abstinence from their teens can best promote this behavior through communication skills—learning to stick up for oneself effectively and communicate what one believes—and by focusing on how to make good choices rather than through simplistic slogans like "Just say no." In her article, Sheely also discusses issues that complicate adolescence for gifted youth, such as asynchrony, social isolation, sensual overexcitability, and androgyny.[22]

The gifted difference is also apparent in gender roles. Research suggests that both highly creative and gifted people tend to be more androgynous than average, meaning that sex-role stereotypes don't seem to apply to them as much as to others.[23] Gifted boys often display traditionally feminine traits and interests, such as nurturance or a proclivity for the arts, while gifted girls often show what we usually think of as masculine traits and interests, such as assertiveness or scientific study.

Androgyny is valuable in creative thought and production because it allows us access to a broader range of the human experience. Parents may need to remind themselves that androgyny is different from sexual orientation, and whether a child is heterosexual or homosexual will not change based on what personality traits and areas of interest the child has. What it means to be a boy or a girl will be different for the androgynous child.

If a teen does indicate that he or she is homosexual, parents can remember that this is another lifelong difference from the norm that the child will experience and that, as with the gifted difference, self-acceptance and understanding are keys to both emotional and sexual health.

Intense and Excitable Families

Do you see yourself in any of the above descriptions of overexcitabilities? Which ones? Are they the same areas as those your children seem to have, or different? Which excitabilities do you find most challenging in your teenagers? Which ones do you struggle the most with in yourself?

Susan Daniels, co-editor of *Living with Intensity*, writes that over-excitabilities "in gifted and highly gifted families create certain social/emotional challenges for the entire family."[24] She writes that these challenges can begin as early as infancy, when an overexcitable baby prefers to soak up the world around him rather than sleep, and continue through childhood, adolescence, and on throughout the lifespan. She concludes:

> *[I]t is essential for the optimal development of gifted children that they learn strategies for self-nurturing and for modulating their overexcitabilities. It is also important that their parents have as much support as possible and the opportunity to refuel their own energy stores.*[25]

If you are reading this book because you have an intense, gifted teen, chances are that others in your family have traits of giftedness and intensity, too. Daniels describes "emotional flooding" as what happens when our emotional reactions to events and feelings are more than we can handle at the moment. We "lose it" in some way—yelling or shutting down or stomping off. When your family is experiencing emotional flooding as a result of emotional excitability, remember that you are affected as well.

Imagine, for example, that you come home to your tearful teenage daughter who is sure that her future is ruined because she got a C on a literature quiz. On a different day, she might see this minor challenge more objectively, but because she has also just broken up with her boyfriend and additionally is preparing for a state swim meet, her emotional responses have overflowed, or flooded. Now imagine that you have your own stressful situations on this particular day—your workplace is announcing layoffs next week, you are worried about housing decisions for your aging parents, and you are coming down with a cold. Your daughter's emotional flooding might very well trigger your own emotional flooding unless you remain aware of what is happening. Instead of yelling, "I can't handle this now!" to your daughter, you can take a deep breath and explain that you need a few minutes to unwind—maybe go for a walk—before you talk about the quiz. Even better, see if your daughter wants to take a walk with you, allowing both of you to work off some emotional energy and giving you a chance to model healthy management of emotions.

Finding support and sources of energy for yourself might mean reaching out to others. Just like your children, you will want to seek out and talk with those who share your experiences. If you have adult siblings who share your intensity, tell them what you have learned. Share stories of how you used to spend hours playing complex imaginary games, and talk about whether your imagination serves you now in your job or interests. You can also look for (or start) a support group for parents of gifted children, where you undoubtedly will meet other intense, overexcitable adults, many of whom struggle with the same issues and problems that you face. Also, do not hesitate to seek professional counseling when life becomes overwhelming or a child becomes out of control or violent.[26]

We all want to be understood and accepted for our differences. Learning about overexcitabilities within the context of the family can help us practice and teach tolerance. Think about your parents. Were they overexcitable in specific ways? Does learning about giftedness and intensity help you to understand them better?

Final Words

Parenting a highly intense child or teenager is not easy. Dabrowski referred to the overexcitabilities as a "tragic gift." I have heard more than one parent complain that it is tempting to say that his child *suffers from* giftedness rather than that he *is* gifted. Maybe this helps to explain how hard it can be, for both child and parent. People who insist that being gifted is a walk in the park don't understand that the park, while beautiful and extensive, is also wild, often pathless, and filled with brambles.

During the difficult times, parents can remember the potential joy and privilege of raising a gifted child—truly, they do exist—and can work to accept their children just as they are. This can be particularly hard for parents whose temperaments differ markedly from their teens or who had very different expectations as to what giftedness looks like. If you imagined that the infant in your arms would grow into a bubbly, popular,

> *I'm too sensitive at times. At other times an atom bomb in the backyard wouldn't faze me. Mostly the small things eat away at me and the big things that hang most people up—like death, nakedness, loss, sex, appearances, luxuries, possessions—don't faze me one bit.* (AAGC, 1978, p. 17)

well-rounded teenager, you will find it difficult to understand how she turned into a "bucket of nerves." Harvard psychology professor Jerome Kagan's longitudinal study of temperament focused on people that he called "high-reactors." In babies, being a high-reactor was measured by "whether babies were easily upset when exposed to new things." A writer for the *New York Times Magazine* explains Kagan's findings:

> *Most of the high-reactive kids in Kagan's study did well in adolescence, getting good grades, going to parties, making friends. Scratch the surface, though, and many of them—probably most of them— were buckets of nerves. "It's only the high-reactives who say, 'I'm tense in school, I vomit before examinations,' 'If we're going on a class trip to D.C., I can't sleep the night before,'" Kagan told me. "They don't like it, but they've accepted the fact that they're just tense people."*[27]

In other words, some people are born highly reactive—or intense, or excitable, or sensitive. It's all okay, and the sooner our children accept whatever their temperaments are as normal for them, the sooner they can learn ways that their intensity can work for them rather than against them and experience full and healthy social-emotional growth.

Recommended Further Reading

Living with Intensity: Understanding the Sensitivity, Excitability, and Emotional Development of Gifted Children, Adolescents, and Adults
Edited by Susan Daniels & Michael M. Piechowski
Great Potential Press, 2009
The collection of articles in *Living with Intensity* covers intensity as it presents itself in all aspects of the lifespan and represents a wide variety of perspectives on Dabrowski's overexcitabilities.

The Mislabeled Child: Looking Beyond Behavior to Find the True Sources and Solutions for Children's Learning Challenges
By Brock Eide & Fernette Eide
Hyperion, 2006
In *The Mislabeled Child*, Doctors Brock and Fernette Eide of the Eide Neurolearning Clinic share their knowledge of brain-based learning challenges and show how parents and teachers can support and help children who struggle with everyday learning, with attention given to how giftedness affects diagnoses.

"Overexcitability and the Gifted"
By Sharon Lind
Available online at www.sengifted.org/articles_social/
Lind_OverexcitabilityAndTheGifted.shtml
Sharon Lind's article is a clear explanation of Dabrowski's five areas of overexcitability and includes specific and general suggestions for parents and teachers of excitable, gifted children. Some of her suggestions include building in time for psychomotor activity before and after more sedate activities; recognizing that some children with sensual overexcitability thrive by being in the limelight, and finding healthy ways to bring that limelight to them (such as putting on informal plays or giving musical performances); and showing children with intellectual overexcitability how to find answers to their own questions rather than simply giving them the answers.

"Mellow Out," They Say. If I Only Could: Intensities and Sensitivities of the Young and Bright
By Michael M. Piechowski
Yunasa Books, 2006
This delightful book is a treasure of information, anecdotes, interviews, and perspectives on the experience of being an intense, excitable young person.

"Dabrowski's Theory and Existential Depression in Gifted Children and Adults"
By James T. Webb
Available at www.davidsongifted.org/db/Articles_id_10554.aspx
James Webb's detailed and accessible article describes the existential depression that occurs because we see "how the world was not the way [we] thought it should be or could be." The article also gives many suggestions for managing depression, interpersonal relationships, and oneself.

Misdiagnosis and Dual Diagnoses of Gifted Children and Adults: ADHD, Bipolar, OCD, Asperger's, Depression, and Other Disorders
By James T. Webb, Edward R. Amend, Nadia E. Webb, Jean Goerss, Paul Beljan, & F. Richard Olenchak
Great Potential Press, 2005
The authors of this well-researched book offer parents and professionals information about how characteristics of gifted children and adults are similar to and differ from learning and other disorders, including guidelines to avoid mislabeling gifted children.

Hoagies' Gifted Education Page: Dabrowski's Theory of Positive Disintegration
www.hoagiesgifted.org/dabrowski.htm
This page of useful links from Hoagies—the "all things gifted" Web page—will lead you to articles, book reviews, and websites devoted to Dabrowski's theories of positive disintegration and the overexcitabilities.

Chapter 4
Social-Emotional Growth and Development

In their article "Depressive Disorder in Highly Gifted Adolescents," Susan Jackson and Jean Peterson share a 17-year-old exceptionally gifted student's poignant experience of not fitting in:

> [I]f every second word you utter, every concept you put forth is mocked or belittled, you start to shut down pretty fast. You are forced into reducing your vocabulary, which effectively jettisons your communicative capacities; you learn to translate according to what seems to be the "common kid code." By and large, I realized pretty quickly that I would never fit into their accepted activities, which predominantly focused on establishing a hierarchy of social and physical power—survival of the fittest, if you will. It just did not interest me to participate.[1]

The experience of not fitting in is often very painful for gifted adolescents. As they reach their pre-teen and teenage years, children become more aware of others' reactions, are more likely to project their current situation into the future, and are more prone to thoughts that spiral out of control. The accumulation of years of feeling different, being teased, wondering if something is wrong with them, and bumping against the "common kid code" can leave teens disheartened. Opting out seems easier than joining in.

Parents are in a unique, though not necessarily easy, position to offer their adolescents a broader perspective of what is important, give them the gift of self-understanding and self-acceptance so that they join in life rather than opt out, and help them to understand and ultimately learn to meet their own social-emotional needs. Annemarie Roeper writes of the importance of having parents who are not only *by* their children's side, but *on* their children's side during this journey toward maturity:

> *I would like to impress parents with the reality of the need of the child and that the first requirement is that there be a bond, a lifeline, between parents and child. In my experience, I have found that the solidity of this relationship is the greatest reason that a child will come through the difficult times to which they are often exposed. No matter how isolated some of the very highly gifted feel, they maintain a healthy Self if they feel that their parents are truly on their side. Many children have told me their parents are their best friends and they could not handle life without them.*[2]

Being on our children's side requires great stores of creativity, patience, energy, and trust:

- Creativity to allow us to see our children's needs as unique and to be flexible in our responses to those needs

- Patience to keep our eye on the long-term, lifelong process of learning to live in the world

- Personal energy to handle the emotional challenges of adolescence without sacrificing our own needs or internalizing our children's struggles

- Trust not only that our children can learn to handle life's ups and downs with confidence and even occasional grace, but that we can be there for our children, regardless of how painful or difficult the obstacles

So what exactly are these social-emotional needs, and how are those needs different for gifted teens? We can start by thinking about what our focus should be during these years of transition. All too often, we consider the teenage years to be primarily ones of preparation for college rather than as an important period of transition to and preparation for adult life.

College Prep or Life Prep?

How does our modern society view a young person's coming of age? While coming of age can be observed and celebrated in religious ceremonies, such as confirmation or bar and bat mitzvahs, or in the form of specific honors and responsibilities, such as becoming an Eagle Scout or getting a driver's license, the coming of age ceremony we share most widely as a society is high school graduation.

Unfortunately, graduation from high school is traditionally tied to academic life and, for college-bound students, preparation for college. The rest of the teen's existence, feelings, dreams, goals, and fears—including getting to know oneself and one's talents, thinking about friendships and other relationships, and gaining skills necessary to adapt to life's continual change—take second seat to the college prep timetable. One author suggests that we begin this timetable as early as the summer after eighth grade. In the article "College Prep: One Mom's Timeline for High School," the author says:

> *Make this the cross-country car trip year. Sample different types of schools: big, small, public, private, East, West, Midwest, South, suburban, rural, urban. Your child needs to "see" himself in the place. As my son said, "Where is my new home?"*[3]

The author goes on to say:

> *Try especially to look at colleges in a part of the country far from home. It's broadening for the child and can be financially beneficial. Colleges seek geographical diversity, and some are willing to pay your child to attend.... This is a good time to remind your child that colleges require him to self-report any misdemeanors or similar (or worse!) marks on character and will take them into account.*[4]

Why the early timetable? The children who are being asked to see themselves in a new home (perhaps across the country in order to get more financial aid) and to behave themselves so as not to hurt their chances of admission have not even set foot in high school! And this is only the beginning. As Michael Winerip, who interviews and recommends potential Harvard applicants, writes, "I see these kids—and watch my own applying to college—and as evolved as they are, I wouldn't change places with them for anything. They're under such pressure."[5]

Now more than ever, the years of high school and even middle school are often thought of primarily as years of college prep. Certainly by junior year, if not before, many college-bound students take on a full schedule of AP classes and tests, standardized testing (including SAT or ACT preparatory classes and tutoring), campus visits and interviews, volunteer hours so as to fill out a high school résumé, participation in extracurricular activities and sports so as to be "well-rounded," and studying to maintain a near-perfect GPA.

Of course, planning for one's future is a good thing, as is thinking about what courses to take and what is required in order to reach one's goals. But should college prep really be a full-time vocation? Young people today, especially gifted teenagers who feel pressured to fulfill their potential sooner rather than later, often say that they have little time for reflection, for imagination and personal discovery, for leisurely reading or sleeping in or even long family vacations—unless they are used to visit potential schools—all of which cut into their college prep career.

What can be lost in this busy schedule is the fact that adolescence is about so much more than preparation for college. It's about preparation for the rest of life, which includes moral, personality, and social-emotional development. Going to the "right" college or even any college right after high school is no sure sign of success. Students who defer college for a year or more to work, travel, or just spend more time with their family do not fall behind in life's big picture. In fact, they may be doing themselves a favor by sidestepping the rat race for a little while. Consider these thoughts from former Presidential Scholars, approximately a decade after their high school graduation:

> *[I am] finally making time to catch up with human relationships, having not had time to get properly socialized.*[6]

And:

> *Much of my difficulty in the job-career area comes from (1) school, school, school—when I was little, what I wanted to be when I grew up was to go to college, and (2) my great diversity of interests. It's a hard thing for those of us who were crammed with so many expectations to even know where we stand after ten years. Now, it's time to try new ways.*[7]

Adolescence is a journey toward the world of independent adulthood, having the knowledge and skills to be comfortable in one's own skin, and finding one's way and place in the world. The difference for gifted teens is that their skins are often uncomfortable, and the expectations and norms of the world are often at odds with their own expectations and experiences.

The Gifted Difference

All people, regardless of ability levels or age, have common social-emotional needs, such as the needs for self-understanding, self-acceptance, and a sense of belonging and community. The hyphenated term "social-emotional" is often used to indicate the interconnectedness of social needs and emotional needs. Self-understanding, for example, is tied to seeing ourselves clearly as we fit in with our family, friends, and the society around us, and feeling that we belong in society depends on accepting ourselves as we are.

One way in which the gifted difference affects social-emotional needs is that, ironically, especially for children who are high achievers, the promise of high potential and the

> *Students in my peer group are jealous about my ability. I do my best to share with them my knowledge and I try to help them whenever possible, but all this is to no avail. (Jealousy stirs teasing—which gets to be a drag.)* (AAGC, 1978, p. 21)

spotlight of awards and honors can actually get in the way of self-knowledge and life skills. Felice Kaufman's longitudinal study of 1964–1968 Presidential Scholars, referenced above, offers valuable insight into what happens to many high-achieving adolescents once they grow up and move beyond the reward system of formal education.

Kaufman surveyed more than 300 Presidential Scholars approximately a decade after they had graduated from high school, when the subjects were between the ages of 26 and 32. A majority of the Scholars said that their gifted programs had been worthwhile, and most of them continued their pattern of achievement, going on to earn college honors and begin promising careers. However, Kaufman also found that many of these same "subjects articulated their resentment of the pressure to achieve and the personal problems that resulted from being in the limelight,"[8] and that when "the time came to leave the formal education system, these subjects were at a loss"[9] in terms of finding an identity and being happy with who they were. Their identity had been "top student," and now the student years were over. Some of them looked back to wish that they'd had more time to enjoy life and relationships along the way. Some started to enjoy other interests for the first time. Some left lucrative careers to choose a slower pace and creative or artistic pursuits. They realized that there are other rewards in life besides academic ones.

Kaufman also found that these "children of promise" were haunted by questions of "the authenticity of the abilities, even into adulthood," and they "expected that their success in high school and President's expectations of them as America's future would necessarily presage continued, almost effortless achievement. Consequently, many equated mistakes and disappointments with failure."[10] In other words, their self-definitions were based on the need not only to achieve as close to perfection as possible, but to do so without having to try very hard.

Adults can be tempted to think that children and teens who are exceptionally bright and academically successful will have all the confidence and intelligence they need to figure out the rest of life. The fact is, learning to live well in this world—to be happy, to have strong personal relationships, to know oneself, and to belong to small and large communities—requires skills, practice, missteps from which we learn, and time. Based on her interviews and research, Kaufman offers this thought-provoking conclusion for parents:

> [G]ifted students need to experience many facets of themselves, not just their academic abilities. Over-emphasis on intellectual prowess and competition for awards can have serious long-term consequences, not only for extraordinarily gifted students like the Presidential Scholars but for students of all ability levels.[11]

For gifted adolescents, internal differences of intensity and excitability, perfectionism, asynchronous development, complexity of personality, and divergent thinking also affect their social-emotional needs. These inner differences come into acute focus in adolescence; these young people are more aware than ever of themselves as individuals, the effects that they have on those around them, and the ways in which they are perceived by others.

Outside factors have an impact as well. Here are a few societal factors that can make it hard for gifted adolescents to experience optimal social-emotional growth:[12]

- Age-based segregation

- Peer and adult pressure to conform

- Lack of understanding about giftedness on the part of parents and teachers

- Focus on the external traits of giftedness rather than the internal experience

- Overemphasis on outward achievement rather than internal growth

- Vicarious parenting—living through or trying to correct our past mistakes and failures through our children

- Little encouragement to live authentically

- Adult preoccupation with providing ideal or optimal circumstances

While adults remember some of these perennial societal pressures from their own childhoods—the pressure to conform, for example—other pressures reflect our current preoccupation with continual assessment, the search for the perfect SAT and ACT scores, and involvement in activities not so much to follow interests, but to build a better college application package. While some students pursue these goals because they truly want to as part of their personal goals, many others may do so primarily because of the unspoken message that, especially for gifted students, it is what is expected of them—it's the only way to fulfill their potential.

In addition to internal differences and external influences, an adolescent's intellectual needs play a large role in social-emotional growth. A defining characteristic of giftedness is the drive to learn, the need to know, and the hunger for understanding and creation. When gifted teens are prevented from exploring the limits of their abilities and potential, they are prevented from knowing and understanding an important part of themselves. They must somehow fit their unique intellectual needs into their self-concept and their ability to relate to others—often a daunting challenge.

Finally, there is one other important, if often overlooked, consideration that can affect how effectively parents meet their teens' social-emotional needs. As parents learn about the unique aspects of giftedness, they may realize, perhaps painfully, that their own social-emotional development has been neglected or misunderstood. They are in the difficult position of trying to help their children understand the differences of their giftedness and how to claim their place in the world as mature adults, while at the same time—perhaps for the first time—understanding and gaining insight into those differences in themselves after having felt out of place their whole lives.

Maturity, Revisited

Parents want to see their children grow into a healthy, independent maturity. Much of what we think of as adolescent social-emotional growth is directly related to becoming a mature adult. But what do we mean by *maturity*? Fruit is mature when it is ripe and ready to be picked. A loan is mature when it is ready to be repaid. We use the word "maturity" to refer to being able to reproduce, as in sexual maturity. We also speak of children who are mature for their age or who act immaturely, meaning that they act older or younger than their age. On the other hand, AARP's magazine for seniors was for many years called *Modern Maturity*, implying that growth and development in the modern era does not stop or come due as early as it once did.

Terri Apter, in her fascinating study of young adulthood, *The Myth of Maturity: What Teenagers Need from Parents to Become Adults*, argues that our culture has made a serious mistake in how we think of maturity: "The myth of maturity is the assumption that being mature means being independent in the sense of being separate or autonomous. It is the myth that young people can only prove themselves by showing that they do not need or want their parents."[13]

Like Annemarie Roeper, Apter believes that it is important for parents to be there for their children, to be on their side. She writes that parents can think of themselves as their teenagers' "emotional coach," urging self-reflection and helping young people to understand themselves better. The challenge for parents is that the teen–parent relationship is different from the young child–parent relationship. Our teenagers no longer idolize us. In fact, they are working hard to form their own identities, often by defining themselves in opposition to us. Their communication skills seem to deteriorate as they sigh, roll their eyes, say "Whatever!" and look at us as if we just flew in from Mars. But that *doesn't* mean they don't need us to be there, and it is up to us not to buy into the myth that they don't.

Some people argue that we coddle teenagers too much today and that in the past, children grew up—grew into maturity—much earlier with no ill effects. While it is true that in the distant past, American teenagers had more personal responsibility at earlier ages—working on farms, finishing school early to take factory or other jobs, getting married and having children often before they turned 20—it is also true that the limits of travel kept them closer to their original homes and families. Even in my parents' generation, my father and uncle lived and farmed on the same ranch where their parents lived. They still live there. My brothers and I, on the other hand, all left home for college at age 18—one stayed in our home state, but two of us went to Iowa and Wisconsin—and now we live with our own families in Arizona, Wisconsin, and

Colorado, while our father continues to live on the South Dakota farm where he was a teenager. While he shouldered the responsibilities of hard work and military service as a young adult, he also was in much closer contact with his parents and extended family, and I doubt anyone thought that taking advantage of this familial support was a sign of immaturity.

As we rethink our ideas of maturity, we also need to be aware of the research suggesting that the part of the brain that controls executive processing—the ability to plan, set goals, organize our thoughts, resist impulses, and consider consequences—might very well be delayed in gifted teens in comparison to their age peers.[14] The frontal cortex is the last part of the brain to mature, and it is the primary region associated with executive functioning development. It is complete when young adults are typically finishing college (early twenties). Although judgment lags behind intellect for all children, the gap may be more apparent when immaturity coexists with verbal prowess. So while they are often capable of advanced intellectual reasoning and study, gifted teens might struggle longer than classmates with the more mundane issues of planning for their futures, delaying gratification, and managing their thoughts. In this case, having parents who are on their side and offering social-emotional support is even more important as adolescents make the long and slow transition to adulthood.

Being a parent who fully supports a teen's road to maturity rather than falling into the trap of the helicopter parent—the hovering parent who simply fixes everything instead of teaching children how to solve their own problems—often requires extra thought, time, and energy. Think of the difference between helping a preschooler learn to tie his own shoes and simply tying them yourself because it is faster. If you tie them yourself for too long, you save time in the short term, but your child loses out on gaining skills and confidence. For teens, the difference might be between spending an extra hour showing them how to make a color-coded binder for assignments, rather than either making the binder yourself because it is faster or expecting them to figure it out on their own. Or, if your teenager is unable to prioritize activities and says "yes" to every opportunity that comes along, you might need to take the time to sit with her and give examples of how to back out of commitments gracefully but firmly. Practice the phone conversation: "I know I had agreed to co-chair the prom committee, but I have too many other commitments that are important to me right now, and I won't be able to help this year." Or help her to word the text of an email that declines an invitation.

If your teen is unreceptive to such explicit guidance toward better organization, you can support him nonetheless by never giving up on the idea that he can learn the skills he needs. Refuse to berate his disorganization or nag him to change, which only sets up a power struggle and makes the issue your discontent rather than his self-growth. It might be tempting to say (yet again), "Your room is a wreck! No wonder you can't find your assignments." However, as parents, we know from experience that such pronouncements don't lead to results (if they did, we would say them only once!). Instead, model planning and organization by talking about how you get through your day: "I've been working on this report draft every night for a week, and now I'm ready to proofread it," or, "I never thought I'd get in the habit of going to the gym every morning, but by using a buddy system, I've finally done it."

Parents can also give their children books that show teens how to be better organized. Two good ones are *Organizing from the Inside Out for Teenagers: The Foolproof System for Organizing Your Room, Your Time, and Your Life*, by Julie Morgenstern and Jessi Morgenstern-Colon, and *See You Later, Procrastinator*, by Pamela Espeland and Elizabeth Verdick. Place the book on your teen's bed or next to her door, then walk away and wait until she brings it up for discussion rather than remind her to read it. Sometimes hearing the same advice from someone else—anyone who isn't their parent—does the trick.

Parenting for Social-Emotional Growth

What role can parents and families play in meeting their adolescents' social-emotional needs as they grow into eventual maturity? In *Growing Up Gifted*, Barbara Clark writes that parents are key in helping children toward integrated growth.[15] Social-emotional needs do not exist in a vacuum, and the family is sometimes the only area in a young person's life where he is seen not just as a student or a worker or a volunteer or a friend, but as a whole person. Because of the differences of intensity, gifted children's needs—even basic needs such as food, sleep, trust, and safety—often require special understanding and support.

High energy levels can fool adolescents into thinking they don't need as much sleep as age peers. While one-fifth of gifted children do seem to require less sleep than average, about the same percentage require even more sleep than average.[16] Similarly, intensity, food allergies, and high sensitivity to tastes and smells can interfere with dietary choices or the desire to eat enough of the right kinds of food. Finally, because gifted children often pick up on subtle cues of judgment, intimidation, and manipulation, they can sometimes feel emotionally and psychologically unsafe in situations that might not pose a similar threat to their friends or classmates.

In addition to providing for basic needs as they pertain to the differences of giftedness, we can develop habits of thought as a family that guide our conversations and choices, and we can spend time thinking about what is most important to us in terms of our family's emotional health. Parents can adopt a mindset and perspective that colors their words and actions, and that eventually shapes the family environment.

As any parent of a teenager knows, adults cannot force a particular attitude or set of skills onto their children. You can tell your teens what household chores you expect them to do, for example, but you can't *make* them do them cheerfully. Especially in terms of motivation to change, nagging or ordering simply do not work to produce lasting compliance and only increase family tension and resentment. Instead, make your expectations clear (that they take out the garbage and mow the lawn, for example), state any consequences (you might connect driving privileges to whether they contribute to household tasks), enforce the consequences with as little emotion as you can ("I know you had wanted the car this weekend, but the grass isn't mown yet"), and model the kind of attitude that you hope to see in them (if you don't want them to sulk, be sure not to do so yourself!). Something that has been helpful for me is to try to treat moody adolescents as I would eccentric relatives who are house guests—expect a basic conformity to house rules, but don't show surprise at puzzling behavior or odd responses to seemingly normal requests.

Ultimately, your children and the passage of time will show you what works and what doesn't. It would be easy to have a set of do's and don'ts that we could follow in specific situations guaranteeing successful resolutions to problems and happy, emotionally healthy families. But that's not how life works, especially for gifted families, which tend to be particularly complex.

Instead, parents can consciously build and provide environments that nurture social-emotional growth by supporting everyone's ambitions and goals without undue pressure to conform and with full acceptance of each individual's self, regardless of achievement or outside measures of success. Here are some ideas that are proactive, practical, and adaptable to your own family.[17]

Practice and Value Self-Care

Psychologist James Webb reminds us: "[H]ow seldom do we teach our children to nurture themselves, to believe in themselves, and to praise themselves for courageous attempts." He urges us to show "caring and respect to them if we expect them to be caring toward themselves and others."[18]

To be able to eventually care for themselves, children need to receive the message that self-care is a good thing. Self-care includes not only taking care of our physical needs, but nurturing and sometimes protecting our emotions, choosing friends wisely and setting boundaries when necessary, respecting and meeting our intellectual needs, gaining self-knowledge so as to know better what our needs are—in short, being our own best friend instead of our own worst enemy.

Can we expect our children to treat themselves this well if they don't see us doing the same? Do our children see us owning and listening to our emotions, or do we keep ourselves too busy and too caffeinated to know how we are feeling? Do we set boundaries with our friends, or do we say yes to every request and answer every phone call, regardless of where we are or what we are doing? Do we model workaholic behaviors? Are we meeting our own intellectual needs, or do we assume that our time for joyful learning has passed and deny ourselves the pleasure of intellectual growth? Do we take time to read, sleep, reflect, enjoy life, play, and recreate? Do our behaviors fit our stated values?

Again, the basic need for sleep is a good example. In an article in *New York Magazine*, "Snooze or Lose," Po Bronson cites research that shows that in the last 30 years, the average amount of sleep for children and teenagers has dropped by one hour per night. What difference does one hour make? How about 15 minutes? A study of 7,000 high school students in Minnesota found that those "who received A's averaged about 15 more minutes sleep than the B students, who in turn averaged 11 more minutes than the C's, and the C's had 10 more minutes than the D's." Another researcher concludes, "Sleep disorders can impair children's IQ's as much as lead exposure." Lack of enough sleep has been linked not only to memory and attention problems, but also to obesity.[19]

In recent years, much research has been done on the advantages of aligning starting times for middle school and high school with adolescents' biological clocks. The advantages go beyond memory retention and grades. In Kentucky, after one school district delayed their start time for grades six through 12 by one hour, not only did students get more sleep and need less weekend "catch-up" sleep, but automobile accidents for drivers ages 17 and 18 fell by 17%, while in the rest of the state where school start times were not delayed, they rose by 8%.[20]

While parents can do little to change the time when high school begins or the amount of homework their children receive, they can make choices as a family that value basic needs. Bronson writes that "before children become overscheduled high schoolers gunning for college, parents start making trade-offs between their kids' sleep and their other needs." We know we have an extra hour or so before everyone *really* needs to be in bed, so we convince ourselves that a few more minutes of television or email or computer games are okay. "As a result," Bronson writes, "sleep is treated much like the national debt—*What's another half-hour on the bill?* We're surviving; kids can, too."[21]

Giving adolescents—especially older teenagers—a strict early bedtime out of the blue is probably not the best answer. What we *can* do is to begin to value sleep as a part of meeting our own needs. Allow your children to see you make the choice to go to bed rather than watch a late night show. Pay attention to how sleep affects your mood, your health, and your overall enjoyment, and adjust your schedule accordingly. Send the message that perfect homework and grades are not worth chronic sleep deprivation.

We can treat other areas of self-care similarly. Our children will notice if we stop our busy morning routine to take the time to eat a good breakfast, or if we say "no" to an invitation because we need alone time on the weekend, or if we take an evening art class because it satisfies our creative need. Not only will such self-care rub off on our children, but it makes us better parents and happier, healthier people. There is no downside.

Model and Support Intellectual Risk-Taking

When our son was in first grade, his school had a spelling program that tested students on vocabulary words. The students took a pre-test and a post-test. After only two or three pre-tests on which he scored 100%, our son quickly decided that acing the pre-test was what he should expect from himself. At the time, he even voiced the belief that being smart meant you knew the material before the teacher taught it! Needless to say, the first time his pre-test score was 98%, he thought he had failed.

Our son's experience is all too common for gifted children. So much of what they know has come easily to them, especially if they aren't provided with the resources and curriculum to challenge their abilities. At ages five and six, many of them have already internalized the idea that if they have to work and struggle to learn, they are somehow failing or aren't as smart as everyone tells them they are. The result is the habit of playing it safe intellectually to avoid all but the best grades and highest scores. When they reach the inevitable point at which playing it safe no longer works—often in college—they may lack the study skills, perseverance, and self-confidence to push through the discomfort and find the joy of intellectual risk-taking.

Playing it safe intellectually happens when we really want to learn something new, take a class, enroll in a program, or make big plans, but we hold ourselves back, not because of reasoned decision making, but for fear of imperfection or of what others might think of us. It happens when students take the easy class that will guarantee them an A instead of the course in their passion area that would engage their intellect. Adults play it safe intellectually when they deny their own gifts, creativity, and talents, fearing that if they pursue their real dreams, they might be called out—by others or by themselves—as egotists or frauds.

If you see that your teenagers are holding back for fear of imperfection, especially in areas that are important to them, ask yourself how you can model intellectual risk-taking. Show your children what it's like to try something new or hard, to falter and try again, and to go through ups and downs while continuing to maintain your sense of self-worth. In doing so, you will also take an important step toward your own social-emotional growth.

Modeling risk-taking can be as simple as learning to cook a difficult recipe and serving the less-than-perfect first attempts, or sending your poetry to a local contest, or finally taking the first awkward steps toward the half-marathon you've always wanted to train for. It can also be as big as going back to college or changing jobs or careers. When we let our children know that we feel hesitancy or even fear in the face of such risks—"I was terrified to take that poetry class, but I'm so glad I took the chance!"—we show them that fear of failure need not be a barrier to pursuing our dreams.

In addition to providing examples of healthy risk-taking, parents can also think twice before commenting on what might seem at first glance to be a failure on the part of their children. For sensitive and perfectionistic teens, a word of encouragement for taking a risk is much more effective than a reminder to try harder next time. Was the less-than-perfect grade really a sign of laziness? Or was it the by-product of intellectual risk-taking and appropriate challenge? Especially at the beginning of learning any new skill, we should expect a certain amount of faltering and clumsiness. As we'll learn in Chapter 5, the willingness to risk mistakes and failure is also necessary for creativity.

Encourage Positive Self-Talk

Spend a day or so paying attention to your self-talk—what you say to yourself in your own head when no one is listening. How much of it is encouraging? *Nice try! That was better than last time. I handled that situation with grace.* How much of it is scolding or negative? *How could I do that again!? When will I ever learn? I am so stupid!*

Also listen to your self-talk about other people: *Here we go again! Bill is so much the favorite; he always gets to do what he wants, but I never do. No one likes me. Nothing in this family is fair.* Translate this to: *I think I'll have a chip on my shoulder for a while.*

It's interesting that the self-talk that slips through to out-loud comments is almost always of the negative variety. We never catch ourselves saying, "That was really well done!" aloud, while we often might mutter, "How could I be so stupid?"

Here are some important and perhaps surprising truths about self-talk: How we think affects how we feel. We can control much (but not all) of our internal chatter. And we can get more control of our self-talk with practice.

All of us—parents and children—talk to ourselves almost constantly throughout the day. Many of us aren't aware of the internal chatter, or if we are aware of it, we feel that we have little control over the content. Yet the dialogue we have with ourselves has a great impact on not only how we feel about ourselves, but how we feel in general.

Here is a thought experiment: Imagine that you step outside on the first really cold day of autumn. Your thoughts go something like this: *Oh, I can't believe summer is over! I haven't taken out my fall sweaters yet. I'm definitely not ready for cold weather.* Do you feel happy? Probably not. Now imagine these thoughts: *What a crisp October day! The colors are beautiful. I'll make myself some hot chocolate when I get home.* Did your emotions change? (If you live in a warm climate, change the text to reflect the hottest day of summer, first thinking negative thoughts, then positive.)

The words that swirl through our head really do shape our emotions. Trying to manage those words is difficult at first—and it's important that we do so without judging the thoughts that we automatically have—but in time and with practice, we really can change the tone of our internal dialogue, which in turn changes how we feel.

Being aware of the words and phrases that we say to ourselves is a large part of changing the subtext upon which our emotions are based. In fact, simply noting whenever we are silently berating ourselves or repeating old, negative scripts makes it much easier to rewrite those scripts in the future. Because our self-talk seems automatic, it's good to have a few positive stock phrases—often referred to as affirmations—to put in their place, so that the next time you catch yourself thinking, *I'm so lazy!*, you can immediately follow up with, *I have an easy-going nature*, or, *I'm going to do the first step now toward my goal*.

Does this sound silly? Is it any sillier than the thoughts that already take up space in our heads? By talking to ourselves as we would talk to a dear friend, we gain a powerful ally in our emotional growth: ourselves.

We can help our children change their negative self-talk by:

- Letting them know that self-talk is normal. Some parents can do this most naturally by bringing up their own self-talk and how it has helped or hindered them. My experience is that a lot of teenagers think they are the only ones who put up with "brain chatter," and they are relieved to know that self-talk is not a sign that they are crazy. I remember, for example, how "sure" I was in high school that I wouldn't get into college—any college. I tell this now to my son, and he laughs with me, but I can see that he also realizes that perhaps his own worries about his future might be just as unrealistic.

- Restating their negative statements about themselves in positive terms. If, after getting a less-than-perfect grade, your perfectionistic teen says, "I'm so stupid," instead of replying, "You're not stupid"—which only reinforces the negativity—you could respond with, "You studied hard for that exam," or ask, "What part of the test did you do well on?" The goal is for them to hear alternative versions of their own self-talk rather than their old scripts repeated back to them, so that eventually they may begin to think differently.

- Encouraging them to record their thoughts in a journal. This could be an online journal, a notebook, or even a video journal—any form that allows them to be candid and that promotes self-awareness. You might buy your teen a nicely bound journal and a special set of pens as a way to start.

- Suggesting yoga or some other meditative practice, especially if that practice focuses on attending to our thoughts. Families can even sign up for classes together. I know one family who goes on an annual summer yoga retreat as their family vacation.

Listen to Emotions

Have you ever felt an overwhelming emotion, but you aren't sure exactly what it is? You might be bursting with something close to joy or rage or fear, but the uncertainty of what you are feeling only adds to the binding strength of the emotion. Or maybe you do know what you are feeling—anxiety, for example—but you seem unable to get beyond it.

The next time this happens to you, take the time to sit with yourself for a few moments—step outside or go into the bathroom if you have to—and examine exactly what you are feeling. Try out different words to see what fits, what feels right. Are you angry or perturbed? Stressed or simply exhausted? Then, try saying to yourself, *I feel _____.* Don't try to change how you feel, just admit it. See if this alone doesn't help to dissipate some of the strong feelings.

Sharon Lind urges gifted adults and children to develop an expanded "feeling vocabulary."[22] She suggests looking up and listing synonyms for some common emotions. For example, suppose your teenage daughter is feeling anxious about upcoming college applications. Here are some synonyms for "anxious" that might help her to understand more specifically how she is feeling: *afraid, aghast, antsy, apprehensive, basket case, bugged, butterflies, careful, choked, clutched, concerned, disquieted, distressed, disturbed, dreading, fearful, fidgety, fretful, hacked, hyper, in a state, in a tizzy, in suspense, jittery, jumpy, nervous, nervy, overwrought, restless, scared, shaking, shaky, shivery, shook up, shot to pieces, solicitous, spooked, strung out, sweating bullets, taut, troubled, uneasy, unglued, unquiet, uptight, watchful, wired, worried sick, wreck.*[23]

Depending on your relationship and your daughter's particular needs, you might be comfortable sharing this list with her and even laughing over some of the possibilities. However, you as a parent can also use the list in your conversations without her knowing that you did any behind-the-scenes work. Your mention that she sounds "spooked" by the idea of the unknown might be just what she needs to hear to crystallize her own feelings.

Encourage Ownership of Excitability and Sensitivity

Teenagers often struggle with understanding what it means to be gifted. Younger children, while they can certainly be aware of their differences from other children, are less self-conscious about how others understand those differences. Older adults bring valuable life experience to their understanding of self, including giftedness. Adolescents, however, are stuck in the middle—aware, sometimes painfully, of their differences, but uncomfortable with labels and resistant to being defined by others.

An article in the online Web journal *ScienceDaily* offers some guidance for parents in helping their adolescents to form a healthy self-identity:

> *[G]ifted youths frequently report social difficulties and the feeling that other children keep distant from them because of the gifted label, and therefore it is important to enable them—in the process of forming an identity—to relate to emotional and social characteristics, such as motivation, self-concept, and external pressures, and not only to those characteristics related to cognitive aptitude.*[24]

I have found that teens sometimes embrace the concept of intensity or excitability (described in Chapter 3) much more easily than they accept the label of gifted. They immediately identify with the intensity of intellectual, emotional, psychomotor, imaginational, or sensual excitability. Being "really smart" is a slippery idea—one that can make them feel like frauds if they don't really believe it or if they aren't at the top of their class. On the other hand, having intellectual excitability that shows itself in voracious reading, puzzle solving, or love of complex thinking speaks to something true about who they are. It feels authentic. It is something that doesn't change based on grades or outside measures of success.

Ownership of who we are—both the parts that we are proud of and that make life easy and the parts that are painful and challenging—gives us the confidence to handle whatever emotions or situations come our way. If we don't take ownership of our own extreme sensitivity, for instance, we will either constantly put ourselves in situations that make us unnecessarily uncomfortable or we will blame others for our discomfort. Expecting others to feel and experience life in the same way we do is a common mistake, leading us to confusion or even anger at others' actions.

For example, if we are used to asking a lot of questions of friends and acquaintances as a way to show support and curiosity about their lives, we might be frustrated when a friend asks us very few questions, and we may therefore attribute the behavior to a lack of interest in us. However, some people are simply uncomfortable with asking personal questions, even of

When your mind feels restrained and boxed in on four sides with superficial teachers, boring school days and no challenge whatsoever, I recommend the world's best antidote. This secret remedy is simply reading. Books truly can open up whole new worlds. I can throw myself, mind and body, into a good book and watch reality slip away. (AAGC, 1978, p. 34)

close friends, fearing that they are prying or invading our privacy. Instead of waiting to be asked about a part of our life that we want to discuss, we can instead dive right in and bring up whatever is bothering us. In this way, we learn to ask for support when we need it rather than attribute motives to others based on how we think or feel.

Whether in interpersonal relationships or for our physical comfort, if we own our sensitivity, without judgment and with understanding, we can plan ahead to minimize difficult situations. We can wear sunglasses to reduce glare, ask for a corner table at a busy restaurant, or give ourselves permission to say "no, thank you" to party invitations that we really don't want to accept. We can also give permission to our children to make such choices for themselves, regardless of whether others completely understand the reasons. Grandma might think it is rude for her grandson to disappear into the backyard after Thanksgiving dinner, but this time alone might be just what he needs to prepare himself for the family activities planned for later in the day. Self-management of intensity and sensitivity almost always means disappointing others at some point, so children can learn early when such disappointments are worth it and when they are not.

At the same time, we must be sure not to use sensitivity or overexcitabilities as an excuse for rude behavior. It's one thing to excuse oneself quietly from a noisy gathering. It's quite another to storm home and force the rest of the family to follow, or to sulk with the expectation that others will simply know what is wrong. By talking through how they make decisions to manage their own emotions and intensity, parents can help their children know how to handle similar situations with grace. For example, if the Thanksgiving gathering includes relatives who have traveled a long distance, parents can talk about how it is important for everyone to try to spend as much time as they can with

Aunt Louise and Uncle Joe, with perhaps plenty of quiet downtime planned for the following day.

Communicate Respect for Differences

A great challenge for gifted people is that their differentness doesn't always show on the outside. They may look as though they should have no trouble fitting in or being successful. After all, they are smart, so they don't need extra help or understanding. In fact, they have it easier than most other people and shouldn't complain. Right?

This common yet unfortunate misunderstanding of giftedness can cause some gifted children and adults to fight back in the only way they can think of: by being critical of everyone else who doesn't understand. Whenever I hear gifted individuals talk condescendingly of others who don't share their intellectual gifts or sensitivity or intensity, I assume that they have some deep and old hurts from being profoundly misunderstood themselves.

As we adults and families learn more about the role of giftedness in our lives, we can use it as a valuable opportunity to show our children a true tolerance and respect for the internal diversity of others. When we learn that not everyone has emotional intensity, for example, not only do we understand ourselves better, but we understand that others are not necessarily acting insensitively on purpose, nor does their lack of intensity mean that they don't care. They simply are not hard-wired in the same way. Their experience of life is different. Once we know more about our own differences, we can understand others' needs and preferences with a more generous spirit.

For example, how do you manage different levels and types of overexcitabilities in your own family? How do you reach a compromise when one person prefers to work in silence because any extraneous noise is a distraction, while another works best with background sounds? Or how do you handle a child's intense emotional reaction to daily news programs when another person in the family is passionate about keeping up with current events? These questions have no pat answers that work for every family, but we can begin by being sure to not assume that one person's reaction is wrong or needs to be fixed—that the person who prefers silence *needs* to learn to tolerate noise, for example, or that someone who prefers background noise doesn't know how to concentrate. When we try to see the world through the lens of others' excitabilities, we open ourselves to new compromises and solutions, especially in our world of advanced technology. After all, that's what noise-canceling headphones, improved stereo earbuds, and Web-based news programming are for.

Most of us are aware of the importance of not only tolerating, but respecting, learning from, and even embracing the marvelous diversity of our population. We can remember that diversity occurs inside people as well—in how we think (diversity of learning styles), how we feel (diversity of intensity), and how we imagine (diversity of creativity). Learning how overexcitabilities affect an individual's comfort, actions, and relationships can help us to understand and be tolerant of others, on the inside as well as the outside.

Learn about Introversion and Extroversion

Another important internal difference relates to how we replenish our personal energy and our preference for solitude or large groups. Gifted individuals are more likely than the population at large to be introverts, and some gifted experts suggest that the incidence of introversion increases with the level of giftedness.[25] Unlike the stereotype, these introverts are not necessarily antisocial or shy loners. They are successful business leaders, professors, sports figures, even public speakers. They do, however, require more time alone or in very small groups than extroverts. Like giftedness, introversion requires careful understanding and management.

How do you know if your teen might be introverted? First, keep in mind that all of us have some degree of introversion and extroversion, and the extent to which we are introverted or extroverted can change with age, especially in middle age. When we speak of being an introvert, what we really mean is being more introverted than extroverted. That said, here are some common indicators of introversion in children and teens:[26]

- Introverts are fatigued by long hours of socializing, even with good friends.
- Introverts give themselves physical distance when in a new situation or in conversation.
- When interrupted, introverts stop talking.
- Introverts prefer a handful of good friends to large groups.
- Introverts need time alone to recharge energy levels.
- Introverts seem to take on a different personality when among strangers or in new situations.

Extroverts, on the other hand, gain energy from socializing and being in groups of people. They might have many people they consider close friends, and they feel uncomfortable when they are alone for long periods of time. They don't mind voicing their thoughts before they are sure of them, and they readily dive into new activities and situations.

Children who are highly creative might show more of a mixture of introverted and extroverted traits, with the ability to focus for long periods of time alone and to gain energy from solitude, while at the same time being quite gregarious in small groups. In young children, this combination—which David Willings calls the "introverted swashbuckler" in his book *The Creatively Gifted: Recognizing and Developing the Creative Potential*—can be confusing to teachers and other children who expect consistency and don't understand the complex personalities of creative learners.

If you have an introvert in your family, you'll want to learn more about the difference between introversion and extroversion and how to support introverts' needs (see the list of recommended books at the end of this chapter). If you yourself are also introverted, you may benefit from new and valuable insights into what makes you tick. If you are an extrovert, learning more about introversion will help you separate your needs from those of your child, as well as to provide an environment that can nurture the entire introvert-extrovert spectrum.

The following guidelines for introverts are adapted from Linda Silverman, director of the Denver Gifted Development Center, and are good for the whole family:[27]

- Introverts are easily embarrassed, so address any mistakes or errors in private and not in front of friends or in groups.

- When beginning a new activity or meeting a new group of people, allow time for introverts to observe from the sidelines before forcing them to participate or to make friends. Let them know that there is nothing wrong with taking their time to get comfortable—to dip their toes in the shallow pool first—and that they shouldn't compare themselves with people who dive immediately into the deep end.

- When possible, give them the option of practicing a new skill privately before performing publicly. An extrovert might have no trouble sight-reading a piano sonata for grandparents, for example, but an introvert would much prefer to practice it first.

- Give them time to think about questions before demanding answers. Email and texting are very good tools for asking questions that might require some reflection because these forms of communication do not demand instant responses.

- Make sure that children have their own space that they control and that they can go to when they need privacy.

- Whenever possible, alert children to upcoming appointments and schedule changes. Again, email is a good way to offer reminders that can be saved for future reference.

Finally, Silverman reminds us, "Respect their introversion. Don't try to remake them into extroverts."[28] Also, we shouldn't expect introverts to *always* act like introverts, or extroverts to always act like extroverts. Making room for diversity of thought and actions goes a long way toward meeting a teenager's changing needs.

Find Opportunities for Mixed-Age Learning and Socializing

The age-stratified world of high school prevents teenagers from seeing how their development fits in with lifespan learning and development. Many teens enjoy and would benefit from more interaction and conversation with adults of all ages, but the constraints of the classroom leave little time for mixed-age learning. Especially for highly gifted teens, spending most of their time in the company of age peers only reinforces how different they are from the norm.

Peter Gray, a research professor of psychology at Boston College, writes that an advantage of mixed-aged learning settings is that children can "scaffold"—that is, they can see where their learning fits in relation to other ability levels and can use the motivation provided by those of higher ability to learn new skills.[29] In a mixed-age homeschool literature and writing group I coached, I saw firsthand how scaffolding can work. The ages of the dozen or so participants ranged from 12 to 18. Students with less developed writing and reading skills learned alongside those whose abilities were more advanced. Some of the students were more creative and divergent; others were more linear and logical. The result was that everyone benefited from the other students' relative strengths. The younger students often pursued much more complex and rewarding activities than they might have otherwise, while the teens challenged each other and realized that they served as role models for the younger children (note that this is very different from asking gifted students to tutor other students as a way to keep them busy).

Parents took turns leading the group, based on their interests and areas of expertise. One parent who was a professor of acting and theater directed the group in a yearly outdoor production of a Shakespeare play. A father who had a law degree led a unit on writing and presenting arguments. And a mother who was an avid and talented scrapbook hobbyist shared her knowledge of how to record family histories. In this way, the mixed ages included adults from whom the children could learn and with whom they could form relationships.

For this kind of mixed-age group to work, adults must work a little harder to present material and suggest activities that can be modified to fit a wide range of abilities. Giving the children as much choice as possible makes it easier for them to choose the right level of challenge. For example, when studying poetry, the adult leader might introduce a variety of poetry forms, such as ballads, sonnets, haiku, blank verse, and so on, and give the students the choice of which form to use for their own original poems. Examples of mixed-age groups include book discussion groups at libraries or book stores (many of which are open to teens), chess clubs, community rather than school sports leagues, theater troupes, and volunteer organizations.

On a smaller scale, having an adult mentor can also be a form of mixed-age learning for an adolescent. High school teachers are often too busy with several classes of students, grading, and administrative tasks to spend much time with individual students, so parents can also look to family members, friends, workers or leaders in the community, or even local college students, especially for the child's passion areas that a parent does not share. For example, if your son is crazy about car engines but the very mention of them makes you yawn, ask a relative or neighbor or local mechanic to spend some time—with or without pay—to be a mentor or tutor, formally or informally. Many gifted teens form close and lasting relationships with adults who think as they do and who share their interests. These relationships and friendships are no less real than same-age friendships.

Admit and Accept Flaws and Mistakes

Barbara Clark advises that adults who are "successful in guiding the gifted adolescent can admit their own inadequacies and meet the gifted student as a person." These adults "care more about understanding problems or miscommunications than about being in charge." On the other hand, those "least equipped to deal with this situation are those who see their role as one of authority that must be preserved."[30]

Fear of not being in charge and losing our authority or control can cause us to not hear what our children are saying or to stifle their real concerns and fears with well-meaning advice or "lessons" from our own past. We might think that our children need us to be in charge by always being a model of right answers and correct behavior and by being a steady and true compass at all times. What they often need instead is for us to show them what it means to be human and that humans are fallible. They need us to admit to making mistakes.

The fastest way to soften the edges of a defensive, prickly teenager is to share a story of a past mistake. The important thing is not to use it as a lesson or tie it to something specific that your child has done. Simply share your experience as though you were talking to an adult friend. If possible, think of an example that, in the end, had positive consequences, either because it caused you to think differently in the long run, gave you a new perspective, or the results weren't as bad as you had imagined. A college professor I know is fond of telling the story of how, as a new teacher, he contested with indignation the claim by his university's library that he had failed to return a book by saying, "I *always* return my books on time." Weeks later, he found the book in his freezer, at the bottom of a stack of frozen dinner boxes, and had to return the cold book with a rather red face.

When you share these kinds of anecdotes, you are showing your child what it's like to live with one's own inadequacies and missteps, and that sometimes being good enough is even better than being perfect. Even if your child doesn't respond right away or in the way you expected, you are making it more likely that she will share her own mistakes and feelings of inadequacy in the future.

Final Words

The message for parents in this chapter can be summed up in three words: You are important. In the words of the authors of *Talented Teenagers*, "[H]ow difficult it must be for American adolescents to learn how to become mature adults, given how little time they spend alone with their parents."[31]

The teenage years can be emotionally challenging for both teens and their parents. Unsure of how to respond to a seemingly new set of behaviors each day, parents can be tempted to focus on what seems easiest to worry about and control: school, intellectual growth, and grades. If our adolescents are getting good grades and good reports from teachers, then they must be doing fine, or so we tell ourselves. Or we buy into the myth of maturity and tell ourselves that by adolescence, we have done all we can, and now it is time for them to struggle on their own and find the answers by themselves.

Alan and Gail Edmunds, authors of "Sensitivity: A Double-Edged Sword for the Pre-Adolescent and Adolescent Gifted Child," offer a different perspective on the teenage years:

> *Given the emotional challenges of the adolescent period...the focus for the education of the pre-adolescent and adolescent gifted child should be on recognizing and supporting the child's heightened sensitivity, or emotionality, rather than merely focusing on curricula learned or talents exhibited. Helping gifted children to face the pressures of conforming to societal expectations, including conforming to sex-role stereotypes, may be the ultimate education for the sensitive child.*[32]

Recognizing. Supporting. Helping. We can't use grades or test scores to know how well we are recognizing our children's changing needs, supporting their sensitivity, or helping them to avoid societal pressure, but that doesn't mean that we shouldn't continue to be there, even—and maybe especially—when it is hard and when we don't have the answers. Once children get to college, as much as we might talk to them on cell phones or chat via video conferencing and spend money for weekend car or plane trips home, they are often far too busy or far away for us to make up for the valuable time we have during their teenage years.

> *If I were a parent, I would try to be aware of my child's needs, and how best to meet them. Being the parent of a "gifted and talented" child, I would have to be especially sensitive to the hardships that giftedness can cause.* (AAGC, 1978, p. 49)

If your bright teenager doesn't take or pass AP calculus, she can always begin with Calculus I in college. If he doesn't apply to all 12 colleges on his original list or go to a $50,000-per-year dream school, he will surely still find one that is a good fit. There are many good teachers, classes, and schools out there to meet our children's intellectual needs. But our teenagers have only one set of parents capable of knowing and supporting them as only parents can, and for that there is no remedial class.

Recommended Further Reading

Teen Success! Ideas to Move Your Mind
By Beatrice J. Elyé
Great Potential Press, 2nd edition, 2007
This delightful book for teens themselves is written by a high school teacher and gives teenagers guidance and information on a variety of social-emotional and academic topics, such as creative thought, self-esteem, solitude, ambition, and courage.

Some of My Best Friends Are Books: Guiding Gifted Readers from Preschool to High School
By Judith Wynn Halsted
Great Potential Press, 3rd edition, 2009
In addition to hundreds of suggestion for books for gifted readers from preschool through high school, this National Best Books 2009 Award Winner also has extensive chapters on the emotional needs of gifted children, including teenagers.

The Hidden Gifts of the Introverted Child: Helping Your Child Thrive in an Extroverted World
By Marti Olsen Laney
Workman, 2005
Website: www.theintrovertadvantage.com
This book is a must-read for anyone who has a highly introverted child or teen. Laney's book about adult giftedness, *The Introvert Advantage: How to Thrive in an Extroverted World* (Workman, 2002), is also valuable "for introverts and those who care about them."

Social and Emotional Development of Gifted Children: What Do We Know?
Edited by Maureen Neihart, Sally M. Reis, Nancy M. Robinson, & Sidney M. Moon
Prufrock Press, 2001
This collection of essays by leaders in the field of gifted education offers a broad and informative perspective on how parents and teachers currently think about social-emotional development. Topics include asynchronous development, Dabrowski's theory of overexcitabilities, perfectionism in adolescence, social-emotional needs of gay and lesbian children, and gifted children with learning disabilities.

Gifted at Risk: Poetic Portraits

By Jean Sunde Peterson

Great Potential Press, 2009

Jean Sunde Peterson uses poetry to offer descriptions of and insights into the worlds of gifted children. Peterson follows each of 63 poems with a prose narrative, in which she offers her perspective as a researcher and clinician.

Chapter 5

The Creative Teen

*[M]any children have an especially strong preference for learning creatively,
learn a great deal if permitted to use their creative thinking abilities,
and make little educational progress if we insist that they learn
exclusively by authority.*

~ E. Paul Torrance[1]

We pay a lot of lip service to creativity in the classroom, but as adolescents enter middle school and high school, the time necessary to acquire the convergent thinking skills required for standardized tests often eclipses any serious study and use of creative thinking. With today's educational focus on using convergent testing to measure achievement and potential, it is more important than ever to understand the creative mind and what we can do to support creative thinking, especially in children and teenagers who prefer to learn creatively. Not only are creative students less preferred by teachers,[2] but their "creative responses" to lack of challenge often result in their being referred for ADD/ ADHD evaluation.[3] Torrance and Goff warn, "One of the first challenges to creativity may be formal schooling."[4]

Divergent Thinking

Divergent thinking generates many different ideas as opposed to one correct idea, and it verges toward unusual or original thought instead of common wisdom. As we learned in Chapter 2, divergent thinking is one way to think about creativity. We also touched on how divergent thinking and convergent thinking work together, and that schools are designed to test and reward convergent rather than divergent thinkers. Now we will explore the idea of divergent thinking more deeply.

Many tests for creativity, such as the Torrance Test of Creative Thinking, look for these aspects of divergent thinking:

- *Fluency*: the quantity of meaningful and relevant responses
- *Flexibility*: the variety of categories of relevant responses
- *Originality*: responses which are unusual or unique
- *Elaboration*: the amount of detail in the responses

To see how divergent thinking manifests itself in everyday life, imagine that your family is going on a vacation and that you have given your two teenagers the task of planning the trip. "Where shall we go, and what shall we do?" you ask them.

- The sheer number of ideas that your child comes up with is an indication of *fluency*. For example, a divergent thinker might rattle 10 or 20 possibilities off the top of her head, while a more convergent thinker will be satisfied with two or three.

- *Flexibility* refers to the range of difference within the responses. A list that covers many different categories—such as hiking, overseas flight, train trips, historical sites, and Disney theme parks—shows more flexibility of thought than a list of 10 items, all of which involve national monuments.

- Unique responses show *originality* of thought. A more convergent thinker might stick to popular ideas that everyone has heard of, whereas a divergent thinker might suggest a destination not usually considered a vacation spot, such as taking a family vacation by swapping homes with a friend or relative for a week.

- Finally, the amount of detail for an idea is evidence of *elaboration*. An answer of, "We could drive to Yellowstone," is less elaborate than, "We could drive to Yellowstone, and on our way there avoid all interstates and stay only in mom-and-pop motels. We should bring our bicycles. I also want to do some boating. Let's all keep sketch books or journals to compare when we return home!"

The Divergent Difference

The difference between convergent and divergent thinkers can be seen in the episode "11001001" from the first season of *Star Trek: The Next Generation*. For the crew's upcoming time off, Captain Picard outlines his own detailed and linear plans: "Well, I have work to finish, then I'm going to put my feet up, turn on my relaxation light, and lose myself in the pages of an old novel. And you? You've earned a rest." His first officer, Commander Riker, replies, "I'm not good at organizing my time off. Something will turn up. It always does."[5]

Divergent thinking has a big impact not only on learning and decisions, but on relationships. Imagine that you, a naturally convergent thinker, are planning a vacation with your friend, whose thinking is more divergent. You immediately research the lowest airfares, the most convenient hotels, and the best package deals for sites and attractions. You use a vacation guide from the library to find the most popular destinations. You put together an hour-by-hour itinerary for the two weeks that you will be gone to save the hassle of having to make plans on the spot. Your planning starts at the beginning and works its way logically from day to day, step to step.

Your companion, however, has other ideas. She wants to take a road trip by car and see how far you get after one week before turning around to come home. She has made a list of several different lodgings along the way, from hotels to bed and breakfasts to camping sites, so that you have a lot of options as you travel, and she is comfortable leaving some nights unplanned so that you can explore for places to stay when you get there. She also wants to bypass many of the popular sites in favor of unusual places that you discover on your own. She plans the trip starting with the parts that interest her most and works outward from there, seemingly unworried about whether it all fits together in any sort of logical sequence.

Unless the two of you each understand that you are using two very different yet equally valuable modes of thinking, your vacation could easily be called off before it ever begins. Lucy Jo Palladino, author of *Dreamers, Discoverers & Dynamos: How to Help the Child Who Is Bright, Bored and Having Problems in School*, describes the tension that can exist between highly divergent and highly convergent thinkers: "The convergent thinker is a natural at critical thinking. Like all humans, she is prone to criticize what she understands the least. So the convergent thinker tends to be critical, even incredulous, of a divergent-thinking process." On the other hand, "Critical thinking does *not* come naturally to the divergent thinker. She does not understand it, and tends to take it personally. She gets defensive when criticized by a convergent thinker. She feels convergent thinkers believe she is not as smart as they are."[6]

This difference in thinking is particularly difficult for younger divergent thinkers. In traditional classroom settings, these children are constantly asked to think in ways that go against their strengths. Their divergent thinking is rarely rewarded and can even lead to interpersonal conflict and power struggles with adults,[7] yet they often are not shown explicitly how to gain more convergent thinking skills so as to succeed academically.

The answer, however, is not to focus on divergent thinking at the expense of convergent thinking skills. Divergence *and* convergence are aspects of creative production. For example, one model of how creative ideas are produced is this: First we become experts in a particular area of study (convergence). Then we mull over what we have learned and give the knowledge time to incubate (divergence and convergence). Often at this point, a solution or new idea will come to us, seemingly from nowhere—the "aha!" moment (divergence). Finally, we must verify our idea and test it against what is true and practical (convergence).[8]

Without convergent thinking, we risk sloppy thinking or "effortless" creativity that leads nowhere. Without divergent thinking, the "preexisting knowledge of an expert can also act as a corset that blocks novel ideas."[9]

> *My great-aunt, pushing seventy…would still be called "gifted and talented." With me, she has almost single-handedly channeled my interest in writing into actual performance. Along with my family, which is a highly literate one, she showed me that if you're willing to work a little, having exceptional skill can open up doors and outlooks onto this absolutely fantastic world of limitless imagination and boundless possibilities—what can only be described as staggering potential. Infinite diversity in infinite combinations, to fall back on* Star Trek *for a bit.* (AAGC, 1978, p. 64)

Parents can help their children to practice and value both divergent and convergent thinking skills. Just as we can be careful not to squelch new or "crazy" ideas, we can also encourage young people to build strong bases of knowledge and to continue to work with and refine new ideas to test their usefulness. For example, if children express interest in baking and love to experiment in the kitchen, we can support their creation of new recipes (and serve as taste testers along the way), while at the same time encouraging them to learn how to follow recipes, to study the chemistry of yeast and baking powder, and to explore the history of different ethnic cuisines. When the first attempt (or two or three) doesn't work, we can urge children to take careful notes of what they did and try again.

Such skills provide important practice in the kind of research and creative development that occur in both school and work.

The Creative Personality

The psychologist Mihaly Csikszentmihalyi (pronounced "chick-sent-me-high-ee") is an expert in creativity and author of several books, including *Creativity, Flow,* and *Talented Teenagers.* He studies creative people who have been able to use their creativity successfully in work and in everyday life to learn what personality traits, if any, they share. His findings can be summed up in one word: *complexity.* More specifically, Csikszentmihalyi has found that creative people have *psychic complexity:* "the ability to move from one trait to its opposite."[10] He describes 10 pairs of such traits:[11]

- *Energetic and restful:* Creative people can have both sustained bursts of energy and deep periods of rest.

- *Intelligent and naïve:* Creative people are both extremely smart about some things and surprisingly innocent about others.

- *Playful and disciplined:* Creative people have both a zany (divergent) and a straight-forward (convergent) side.

- *Fanciful and reality-based:* Creative people have one foot in the clouds and the other on the ground.

- *Humble and proud:* Creative people are not driven by their egos and may even shy from publicity or recognition, but they also accept and are glad for their gifts and accomplishments.

- *Masculine and feminine:* Creative people exhibit traditionally male and female traits, such as assertiveness and tenderness (note that this dimension has nothing to do with sexual preferences).

- *Rebellious and conservative:* Creative people sometimes are not afraid to break with the status quo and at other times stick with tradition.

- *Passionate and objective:* Creative people can fall in love with the world while still seeing the world as it is.

- *Suffering and blissful:* Creative people know and feel suffering without losing a sense of joy and wonder.

- *Introverted and extroverted*: Creative people are comfortable being by themselves but can also learn and use skills of interdependence.

Psychic complexity—the ability to move between these pairs of traits—allows us to view life from a new and different perspective and gives us a wide range of responses, choices, and skills as we approach problems and goals. For a better of understanding of how psychic complexity works, let's look at one pair of traits more closely: *playful and disciplined*.

Csikszentmihalyi alternatively refers to the traits of *playful* and *disciplined* as *irresponsible* and *responsible*. He quotes physicist Hans Bethe on what allows him to solve the most difficult of physics problems: "Two things are required. One is a brain. And second is the willingness to spend long times in thinking, with a definite possibility that you come out with nothing."[12]

We probably already think of playfulness as an aspect of creativity. Bethe's words help to explain the role of irresponsibility. Parents of teenagers are understandably concerned about helping their children learn skills of time management and personal scheduling—and we will explore their importance in the next chapter—but we can sometimes stop to ask if we make room in our children's lives and give them permission to be playful and, yes, even at times irresponsible. Being willing to "waste" time thinking seems a luxury these days, but perhaps we should view it as a necessity for creative thought.

Another way to understand these traits is to use what we've learned about divergent and convergent thinking. Playfulness often includes divergent thinking—keeping possibilities open, valuing quantity of ideas and experiences before judging their quality, and starting in the middle instead of at the beginning. Discipline, on the other hand, is the linear, step-by-step work of convergent thinking—moving deliberately from step A to step B to step C—and thinking critically about the quality of our work along the way.

If you've ever had the experience of working very persistently and diligently on a task or problem, only to have the answer come to you when you are relaxing or playing sports or even sleeping, you have experienced the benefit of moving between discipline and playfulness. Likewise, if you have ever thought of a creative idea while having fun— on vacation, perhaps, or while taking a walk or listening to music—and later put in long, hard hours to make that idea a reality, you have moved from playfulness to discipline.

If you have a teenager who is already complex in this area, you might be frustrated by his seeming inconsistency. He works hard and plays hard, and you are concerned that he will burn himself out. Parents of such children are often frustrated when the desire for playfulness occurs when you expect or want responsibility, or when your teens decide to bury themselves in disciplined work at inconvenient times for the family or for long periods. The next time this behavior confounds you, stop to think if—in the long run—your child is showing a balance of extreme work and play, one that fits with his own need for creative thought and production.

Of course, some of us are more playful—or more disciplined—than others, but Csikszentmihalyi urges everyone to work toward greater psychic complexity by strengthening and consciously using our weaker or less preferred trait. Playfulness without discipline results in a lot of great ideas that are never realized, while discipline without playfulness results in work that is finished but dry and lacking in creative spark. A teenager who struggles with discipline can use some of the ideas in the next chapter to add more convergent thinking in areas of her life that are important to her, while someone who has a hard time being playful and who deals with a bit too much perfectionism can practice some purposeful irresponsibility—by occasionally stopping when work is "good enough" rather than when it is perfect—for the sake of creativity.

Think about the dimensions of complexity that your children already have, and ask yourself how you can support and better understand them. Then think about the ones in which they are more lopsided. What can you do as a parent and family to show that you value psychic complexity? As always, think of how your own experiences, successes, and disappointments might affect how you react to or support your children.

As co-author of *Talented Teenagers*, Csikszentmihalyi writes that adults who have lingering regrets about their own career choices or who feel stuck in unrewarding jobs "will tend to see interest and effort, play and work, as separate realms because that is how they normally experience them in their own lives."[13] Similarly, parents who feel an unreasonable fear of the playfulness that they see in their teenagers and who jump to unreasonable conclusions that such playfulness will inevitably lead to a life of dashed hopes and lack of self-discipline might be reacting to some deep-seated regrets and fears within themselves. A parent who continually struggles with issues of organization and self-discipline in terms of schedules, for example, might nag children unnecessarily about the dangers of giving into one's impulses or putting fun work before drudgery, without seeing whether or not the children really need such reminders.

The good news is that it is never too late to add more complexity and creativity to our lives. Csikszentmihalyi offers these suggestions:[14]

- Notice something new every day.

- Do something every day that is not what you would usually do.

- Follow where your interests lead you.

- Remember that becoming good at something will make it more fun.

- Think of ways to make your usual activities more complex.

- Schedule time to daydream.

- Be honest with yourself about what you do and don't like about your life.

- Do what you like more often and what you don't like less often.

- Don't stop at your first or easiest ideas; push yourself to think of more ideas, different ideas, and unusual ideas.

Creativity and Flow

Creative persons differ from one another in a variety of ways,
but in one respect they are unanimous: They all love what they do.
It is not the hope of achieving fame or making money that drives them;
rather, it is the opportunity to do the work that they enjoy doing.
~ Mihaly Csikszentmihalyi[15]

In addition to his work on dimensions of creativity, Mihaly Csikszentmihalyi is most well known for his theory of *Flow*. Flow is what he calls a state of "optimal experience." When we are in Flow, we are fully engaged. We lose the weight of self-consciousness. We are working to meet the challenges of whatever we are doing, but we don't feel as though we are working. Rather, we are playing with intensity. Our skills are perfectly matched to the challenge before us.

Flow can happen in a wide variety of areas and activities. Runners experience Flow when they are pushing the limits of their endurance and training and suddenly lose track of time and space, aware only of their muscles working together and moving in concert. Chess players experience Flow when their skills and study allow them to see the upcoming moves play out in their head, when they are guided by their own internal grandmaster. We can even experience Flow in friendship, when our work and time invested in knowing and relating to another person pay off in an ever growing, mutually satisfying relationship in which we lose ourselves temporarily by sharing who we are with another.

Flow doesn't just happen because we want it to. Flow occurs when we are involved in some endeavor outside of ourselves that we have some skills for. A child learning to play the piano, for example, has little chance of experiencing Flow while learning to read notes or how to place his hands on the keyboard. However, with enough practice, his skills increase to the point at which he can play a song; then he has the chance to lose himself in the music that he has learned to make. When that music becomes too easy to produce Flow, he continues to learn and practice so that more difficult challenges are met with ever-improving skills. That's how Flow works. As we get better, we enjoy ourselves more.

Csikszentmihalyi argues that adding more moments of Flow to our lives not only helps us to be more creative and successful, but more important, it makes us happier and improves the quality of our lives. The happiness of Flow is not the fleeting pleasure of a favorite meal or hot shower. It's the accumulation of moments of "optimal experience" that help us feel at one with the world. We have both greater self-knowledge and less self-consciousness. We also gain the long-term joy of personal accomplishment.

> *Photography is stimulating. Every time the camera shutter opens, the picture is always slightly different. My mind is blank to the world; my prime connection with reality is the view-finder. I relax.* (AAGC, 1978, p. 36)

The Creative Home

The authors of *Talented Teenagers* tell us that adolescents who experience the most Flow come from families who offer a combination of support and challenge, and who offer a "supportive context for the development of genuine interests."[16] Parents of these families "reported more rewards from family interaction, more harmony with their spouses, more personal life happiness, and greater expectations for intrinsic motivation in their offspring's career."[17]

Compared to schools, the business world has been ahead of the curve in recognizing the value of creative thinking. Business and trade magazines routinely feature advice for how workers can enhance their creativity on the job by using creative thinking strategies. Many of these ideas are highly adaptable to the home as ways to support children's divergent thinking and challenge them to tap into their creativity more often. Children and adults who are naturally creative can use these techniques to enhance and sharpen their creativity, and others can use them to improve their creative skills. Creative thinking exercises are also a lot of fun and a good way to relax, especially after a long day of convergent work or study.[18]

> *How have my parents helped me in my growth and development? They exposed me to different cultural activities and to many kinds of people and situations. They gave me a home with books, music, movies, and the like; they stressed academics. Most of all, they have watched over me and come whenever I needed them, always with good humor and affection. I was encouraged to pursue any of my interests.* (AAGC, 1978, p. 48)

Parents can spend some time thinking and talking about how they can best challenge their children to find and fulfill their dreams without putting undue pressure on them to do so too early or for the wrong reasons. Finding this balance depends on individual personalities and family circumstances and is often a matter of trial and error, as we make adjustments in our reactions and approaches and as we pay attention to the effects that our words and actions have on our children.

What follows are some ideas for "remodeling" your home to make it more nurturing of creativity. For even more ideas and resources, see the recommendations for further reading at the end of this chapter.

Watch for Genuine, Internally-Motivated Interests

Encourage your children to recognize their genuine interests, and support those interests as fully as possible, even if they aren't traditional school subjects or if they don't seem to lead to a college major or career. Adults and teenagers both can read Ken Robinson's book *The Element: How Finding Your Passion Changes Everything*, which offers an excellent and inspiring argument for doing not only what we are good at, but what we love. Robinson's interviews and examples are drawn from a wide variety of activities and careers, from the Beatles and Warren Buffet to Arianna Huffington and Richard Feynman.

Encourage Broad Interests

Creativity researchers Robert and Michele Root-Bernstein have found that "creative breadth" is an overlooked aspect of creativity: "[M]ost scientists have traditionally focused on a person's main creative endeavor—Mozart's music or Picasso's art, for example. The truth is, however, that most highly creative people are polymaths—they enjoy and excel at a range of challenging activities. For instance,...nearly all Nobel Prize winners in science have at least one other creative activity that they pursue seriously."[19] Many of the most creative and happiest college engineering students who were enrolled in my writing classes made time for intense hobbies—especially for music—in their otherwise daunting course load. Parents can encourage their children to give similar interests and pursuits a high priority in their schedule, even if they don't "count" toward a major or career.

Deemphasize the Importance of Grades and Test Scores

Teresa Amabile writes in *Growing Up Creative* that when children become focused on grades and other extrinsic motivators and measures of success, they are at risk for the "Performance Syndrome."[20] Performance Syndrome occurs when looking smart and not making mistakes are more important than learning and doing one's best. For students with perfectionistic tendencies in particular, Performance Syndrome quickly saps the joy from learning, increases anxiety, and can even lead to plagiarism or other forms of academic dishonesty.

Emphasize Internal Motivation, Planning, and Effort

Instead of praising children for being smart (something they have no control over) or for getting good grades (something they may or may not have worked for), we can acknowledge when they heed their internal voice, when they make plans and goals (especially written ones), and for the effort they put forth.[21] We can also point out when they create moments of Flow for themselves. This doesn't have to sound as awkward or stilted as it might seem. It's simply a matter of saying, "I'm really happy that you decided to try out for the play this fall, because I know it's what you want to do," or, "You worked very hard to learn the material for that chemistry test," instead of saying, "The fall play will look great on your college application," or, "It's good you got an A in chemistry."

Avoid Squelching or Criticizing New Ideas

One of the rules of traditional group brainstorming is the "no squelching" rule. When group members are coming up with initial ideas to solve a problem, no one is allowed in any way to squelch those ideas. Evaluating the ideas and assessing their practicality come much later, once a long list of ideas has been made. If the ideas are evaluated too early in the process, people are less likely to contribute new, possibly off-the-wall ideas that might eventually spark someone to realize the ultimate solution to the problem.

If adults are (with good intentions) in the habit of helping their children realize how every word or thought can be improved, children—especially sensitive adolescents—quickly learn that it's better not to mention any new ideas at all or show their parents any of their work. I've seen this happen often with writing. A child shows her parents a story that she has written, and almost without thinking, the adults note corrections of spelling or grammar or that the beginning seems rough. What new ideas need in their infancy, however, are recognition, acceptance, and time to grow. Parents and teachers can instead say, "You have made me very interested in these characters, and I am curious what happens next. What are some ideas you have?" There is time later for correction and revision, after the initial creative period has played itself out.

To see how the "no squelching" rule can work in everyday life, let's return to the example of planning a family vacation. Instead of asking for practical ideas, ask your children to give you their ideas for the perfect vacation, regardless of cost or travel or other limitations. One idea might be to go back to the time of the dinosaurs. Instead of dismissing this as impossible, you might talk about how much fun that would be, then use this ideal (if impractical) suggestion as a way to plan a trip to a dinosaur dig or to the Chicago Field Museum of Natural History or to a place where dinosaur bones are visible. Edward de Bono calls this technique "Wishful Thinking," because it allows us to come up with new and useful ideas that we would otherwise squelch as impractical.[22]

Put Expectations on Hold and Accept Inconsistency

One of the ways in which we stifle the complexity that is part of creativity is by expecting ourselves and others to be consistent in action and personality. In families, we do this by referring to children as types, such as "the smart one," "the funny one," or "the imaginative one." Without intending to, we give children the unspoken message that their personalities are already fully formed, and they would go against expectations if they behaved or expressed interest in ways that are different from what we expect.

Parents can encourage their children to explore all aspects of personality, and thus enhance their psychic complexity, by themselves doing the unexpected once in awhile. A father who usually is very serious and literal minded can buy himself a comic book, or a mother who is known for her dislike of schedules can, for one day, make an hour-by-hour list of what she plans to do. Families can even plan for "do the opposite" days, in which everyone consciously tries being different from usual or from what people expect from them.

Practice Skills of Goal Setting and Time Management

What do goal setting and time management have to do with creativity? Without the skills to record their goals, to set realistic timetables for getting from A to B, and to manage the 24 hours in every day, gifted children are easily lured by instant gratification to do what comes easily to them. The problem is that what comes easily for them is often, in the early grades, enough for them to get by or even to excel. However, because they aren't developing the higher skills necessary for optimal experience, the level of challenge will be too low for them to experience the creative Flow experiences described by Csikszentmihalyi.

Many creative people need specific instruction and practice in order to learn how to manage their time and work, not only because they might prefer divergent thinking, but also because, if they are academically gifted as well, they have little outside incentive to obtain these skills. When that happens, they can enter high school or college unprepared to do the work necessary to meet their dreams.

For example, suppose your daughter is a gifted writer who can easily get an A on an essay by writing it the night before. While other students begin their papers several days ahead of time because they know that they will need to edit and rewrite in order to do well, she waits until the last minute. While she might get a brief adrenaline rush from working on such a tight deadline, she misses out on the rewarding process of writing and rewriting, using great care to find exactly the right word or to say exactly what she means, and then rewriting more to make it even better. When she does receive her A, she knows that she didn't really earn it, so joy in completing a difficult and challenging task is once again lost.

On the other hand, if she learns to value the process of study and work for the right reasons, she can become better as a writer and challenge herself to more creative and difficult writing tasks. Ideally, of course, teachers are a part of this process, as they recognize and encourage students who need greater challenge. But even if your child's classroom does not provide this challenge, you can offer a home environment that encourages work and diligence for the sake of personal satisfaction.

Recommended Further Reading

Creativity: Flow and the Psychology of Discovery and Invention
By Mihaly Csikszentmihalyi
Harper Perennial, 1997
Based on 30 years of research and 91 interviews of world-renowned creative people, *Creativity* contains Csikszentmihalyi's full theory of Dimensions of Complexity, with many examples and a chapter on enhancing personal creativity.

"The Creative Personality"
By Mihaly Csikszentmihalyi
www.psychologytoday.com/print/21439
This online article from *Psychology Today* is a clear and shortened discussion of Mihaly Csikszentmihalyi's Ten Dimensions of Complexity. If the link above doesn't work, go to www.psychologytoday.com and search for "The Creative Personality."

"Seeing the Ordinary as Extraordinary"
By Dewitt Jones
www.dewittjones.com/resources/seeing_the_ordinary.htm
Dewitt Jones, a National Geographic photographer, offers clear and empowering advice for how to see and live life in a more creative way. The article is based on his DVD titled *Everyday Creativity*. Look for the DVD in your local public or university library.

Different Minds: Gifted Children with AD/HD, Asperger Syndrome, and Other Learning Deficits
By Deirdre Lovecky
Jessica Kingsley, 2004
Different Minds is an excellent resource for parents of creatively gifted children who struggle with the structure and expectations of traditional classrooms, regardless of whether they have diagnosed learning deficits.

Dreamers, Discoverers & Dynamos: How to Help the Child Who Is Bright, Bored and Having Problems in School
Lucy Jo Palladino
Ballantine Books, 1999
The title of this book says it all (its former title was *The Edison Trait*). Lucy Jo Palladino describes in detail workings of the young divergent mind and offers specific steps for helping divergent thinkers to use their creativity to their advantage and to handle classroom learning.

Understanding Creativity
By Jane Piirto
Great Potential Press, 2004
Jane Piirto's book is an excellent overview of not only theories of creativity, but what creativity looks like in specific arts, sciences, and other disciplines. She also includes useful and practical suggestions for how parents and teachers can enhance children's creativity.

Mind-Mapping
www.buzanworld.com/Mind_Maps.htm
Tony Buzan's technique of mind mapping is a visual, non-linear way to think through, record, and connect. Many of my college students find it an effective way of taking notes, planning essays, and studying for tests. Visit Tony Buzan's website to learn how to Mind Map and to see several examples.

TED Talks: Ideas Worth Spreading
www.ted.com
TED (Technology, Entertainment, Design) Talks is an amazing, free collection of lectures on creativity, invention, the future, and almost any important big idea that you can think of by people like Bill Gates, J.J. Abrams, Jeff Bezos, Michelle Obama, and Jane Goodall.

Chapter 6

The Self-Directed Teen

Wanting to "do it myself" is a hallmark of young gifted children. During early childhood, parents of intense children watch with awe and perhaps envy as other preschoolers allow their parents to direct them in matters big and small, from picking out their clothes in the morning to telling them when to get ready for bed. Compliant, however, is rarely the first word that adults think of to describe a typical young and strong-willed gifted child who seems to live by the motto "You aren't the boss of me."

When parents first begin to understand what makes their intense child click, they are often surprised to learn that self-determination is one of the defining characteristics of giftedness, and not something they caused or even should try to fix. Deirdre Lovecky lists self-determination or "entelechy"— a Greek word meaning having one's

> *In looking back on the culmination of events [of my life], I am thankful and can say, "I did it my way." I have learned that you only get out of life what you put into it. How true the saying is. I can see where I put miles of effort into my pursuits. I can see where I put little or no effort forth. And the results correspond every time. (AAGC, 1978, p. 14)*

end or fulfillment within—as one of five traits of gifted children, the others being divergent thinking, excitability, sensitivity, and perceptiveness. She describes entelechy as "a particular type of motivation, need for self-determination, and an inner strength and vital force directing life and growth to become all that one is capable of being."[1]

Self-determination or self-directedness is connected to other aspects of giftedness. Intense curiosity or intellectual excitability is inner directed rather than assigned by others. Divergent thinking shows itself as a desire to go in new or different directions. The joy of Flow requires that one works toward a personal goal that is meaningful. In other words, the inner drive to ask, to learn, and to create is part of the gifted difference.

Just as intensity and overexcitability can be painful as well as joyful, the drive of self-determination does not always make life easier and can lead to internal and interpersonal conflict.[2] Feeling driven to accomplish tasks that one is not ready or allowed to do can cause great frustration. Especially in school, self-determination can lead to confrontations with teachers and other adults who insist that children are not old enough or informed enough to know what or how they should learn.

Like intensity and overexcitability, self-determination does not go away as gifted children grow up. Mary Elaine Jacobsen lists three main traits of gifted adults as intensity, complexity, and drive. In her book *The Gifted Adult*, she describes both positive and negative aspects of drive:

> *[It is] the goal-orientation of a self-starter who pushes toward perfection; one who feels an inner sense of urgency and can feel shattered when an important dream seems to fall apart; one who looks for security in systems, rules, and order; one who struggles with self-doubt and high standards; a big picture trail blazer who is driven by a sense of personal mission.*[3]

A goal for gifted adults, a topic which we will explore in Chapter 8, is to learn to use their drive in a balanced way for personal fulfillment, without its being either collapsed into apathy or exaggerated into an "unmanaged drive" that can "swallow us whole." Not until middle age are many gifted adults ready to understand their drive fully or to use it most effectively.[4] Certainly in the teenage years, self-determination can feel like an unbroken horse, ready to gallop to distant pastures but without direction or discipline.

Self-Determined Teens

Between the obvious "I wanna do it my way" years of early childhood and the more conscious, more deliberate use of self-determination in adulthood lies the transition period of adolescence. As with so many other traits of giftedness, self-determination often presents itself in extreme and challenging ways during the teen years.

The self-determination of some high school students is impossible to miss and is highly valued by adults. These teenagers manage their education and career plans with the force of CEOs. They juggle a schedule that leaves their parents dizzy. They know exactly where they want to go and who they want to be. When I think of this kind of student, I am reminded of a young man I know whose goal in high school was to attend The Juilliard School in New York to study acting, a program that admits only about 18 students per year. Day in and day out he worked toward his dream, always prioritizing his time with his goal in mind, fitting in as many local theater performances as he could in a busy schedule of school and work, seeking mentors in a local theater academy who could prepare him for what to expect at auditions. No doubt, many adults and even friends, while rooting for him, thought his dream improbable, if not impossible. However, today, as I'm writing this chapter, he is a freshman in Juilliard's Drama Division.

A strong self-determination can also show itself in ways that garner less public acclaim or follow a less traditional path to success, but nonetheless fulfill personal goals. For example, a student who opts out of school-sponsored activities or honors classes to gain free time to practice rhythm and blues guitar for hours every day and learn all there is to know about Robert Johnson and the history of American blues guitar music is no less self-directed than a student working to get into Juilliard. The difference is that others might not recognize the self-determination in the guitar example as valuable or useful when compared to the student who got to Juilliard.

Other teens seem to want to be self-directed but are unable to do so, much to their own frustration and that of the adults around them. They seem incapable of keeping their papers organized, setting schedules for themselves, or following directions, even for projects and interests that are meaningful to them. They have trouble breaking large goals into small tasks. They may be very creative or have learning differences that prevent their self-determination from working to their advantage.

Finally, self-determination might seem to disappear entirely for awhile in some teenagers as it takes the form of what Herbert Kohl calls *active not-learning*: willing oneself not to learn something that one is expected to learn, a process that "can require actively refusing to pay attention, acting dumb, scrambling one's thoughts, and overriding a curiosity."[5] Kohl explains that children choose not-learning, not because they are unable or don't want to learn, but as a form of self-determination and control. He writes of "obviously intelligent students" who accept their abilities but choose not to use them as others want them to:

> *They had consciously placed themselves outside the entire system that was trying to coerce or seduce them into learning and spent all their time and energy in the classroom devising ways of not-learning, short-circuiting the business of failure altogether. They were engaged in a struggle of wills with authority, and what seemed to be at stake for them was nothing less than their pride and integrity.*[6]

This form of self-determination is so strong that, in Kohl's words, "to learn from a stranger who does not respect your integrity causes a major loss of self"[7]—a loss that the student is not willing to suffer. Not-learning might also be a way for children to get back at parents whom they feel are pressuring them about grades, or as a way to draw attention to themselves in difficult family situations such as illness or divorce.

As we can see, self-determination can take many forms during the adolescent years. Students who are not organized and seem directionless do not necessarily lack drive and motivation. Often they just need adult support, skills of self-management, practice, and patience for their self-determination to surface and flourish.

Asynchronous Development and the Gifted Difference

As we learned in Chapter 2, many people mistakenly think that asynchronous development goes away or evens out during the teenage years. The reality is that adolescence can bring uneven development into sharp focus as intellectual abilities soar past social and emotional skills. As mentioned earlier, research suggests that one area in which gifted teens may experience uneven growth in comparison with age peers is in the area of executive functioning.

Executive functions include "planning, goal setting, organizing thoughts, suppressing impulses, and considering consequences before acting."[8] Executive functions are thought to be controlled by the brain's frontal lobe. In all children, this is the last part of the brain to mature during the slow process of refinement of neural connections, a process that occurs roughly from age five to 20 or even later.[9] Until the frontal lobe is mature—that is, until the brain change is complete—adolescents are likely to make judgments based on emotion rather than reason and to fail to take into account long-term goals when making short-term decisions.[10]

Here again we find a gifted difference: While adults might expect brighter students to have more mature judgment at an earlier age than their classmates, the reverse can be true. Judy Willis writes in *Inspiring Middle School Minds: Gifted, Creative, and Challenging* that recent research using functional Magnetic Resonance Imaging (fMRI) suggests that "frontal lobe maturation in gifted students appears to be delayed even longer than in their age-matched classmates."[11] Other findings suggest that the more highly gifted a child is, the later this process begins. While more research is needed to understand fully how this process works and what its implications are, the important point is that the judgment capability of gifted teens may be inherently different from that of their classmates.

Nadia Webb, a neuropsychologist and co-author of *Misdiagnosis and Dual Diagnosis of Gifted Children and Adults*, explains the difference succinctly: "Phenomenal intellects can coexist with mediocre executive functioning skills."[12] She writes that some gifted children might do fine with short-term tasks but struggle with long-range projects that require skills of "planning, judgment, self-monitoring, and organization," since these are "the last skills to mature developmentally."[13] Even more so than other teenagers, gifted children may need specific, step-by-step guidance and adult scaffolding for a longer period of time to help them meet their goals and handle a normal workload.

Consider a high school freshman who is taking pre-calculus and who scored well enough on standardized tests to qualify for gifted summer programs, but who routinely gets C's or lower because he loses track of assignment sheets and can't manage his study time. Rather than assume that he simply should know better given how smart he is— which is an unfortunate but common assumption—we can ask if he is experiencing the asynchronous development of someone who is intellectually advanced in specific areas but whose organizational and self-monitoring skills need more support than the average freshman. He might benefit from school programs that help with organizational or study skills, for example. Many gifted high school and college students mistakenly think that such programs are not for "smart" students. The truth is that even gifted adults often need to reach out to others to learn how to plan more effectively and follow through on tasks. Alternatively, a parent could take the time to sit with the teen to plan a study schedule and to show him how to build in incentives to prod him gently toward his goal. For example, he might reward himself with a favorite video game after he completes an assignment or treat himself to a new music download after getting a B or better on an exam. Or he could do his homework in a common yet quiet area of the house instead of his room, not so that he could be monitored so much as for moral support.

The goal of this guidance and scaffolding is to give students the tools and confidence they need to be self-directed learners. While many gifted people are naturally driven and self-propelled to learn and to follow their own paths, they don't always know how to manage this self-direction. For example, our math whiz, above, is self-directed when he chooses role-playing games instead of studying for a test, but it's a self-direction that, in the end, is not necessarily in his best interest. Before we look at some ways to help young people with skills of self-management and to encourage them to use their self-determination in healthy ways, let's first look at what we mean by "self-determination" and "self-directed learning" and why self-directed learning is important.

Recognizing Self-Determination and Self-Directed Learning

We can think of *self-determination* as acting under one's own free will and being in charge of one's own mind and life, without undue outside influence. The phrase self-determination is often used politically to refer to countries that are independent and self-governing, as opposed to being colonized. Everyone has some degree of self-determination; how-ever, the self-determination inherent in giftedness is stronger than usual and shows itself at an earlier age.

Self-directed learning refers to an educational philosophy that sees the student—whether child or adult—as an active, self-determined learner. Cheryl Lowry writes that being in charge is at the heart of self-directed learning:

> [S]elf-directedness depends on who is in charge—who decides what should be learned, who should learn it, what methods and resources should be used, and how the success of the effort should be measured. To the extent the learner makes those decisions, the learning is generally considered to be self-directed.[14]

Self-directed learners not only learn because they choose to, but they also accept responsibility for their learning by taking initiative, assessing their progress, and making changes when possible. This is not to say that self-directed learners work in isolation. They work with teachers and mentors and anyone else who can help them learn. The difference is that their teachers no longer control the entirety of what, when, and how they learn.

Here are some ways that learners show self-direction:[15]

- When they decide what they need or want to learn

- When they set their own goals

- When they identify and find resources for learning (including teachers and mentors)

- When they choose and use strategies for learning

- When they evaluate their own learning

Another way to think of self-directed learners is as "autonomous learners," a phrase used by George Betts, professor of gifted and talented education and co-author of *The Autonomous Learning Model*, a learning program designed to help gifted students become self-directed learners. Betts writes that an "autonomous learner, by definition, is one who solves problems through a combination of divergent and convergent thinking, and functions with minimal external guidance in selected areas of endeavor."[16] This complex combination of divergent and convergent thinking is also indicative of creative learning. An example of how self-directed learning can work in the classroom is the Autonomous Learning Model's dimension of In-Depth Study, in which students choose an area of passion or high interest, design a project or unit, share it with others, and finally evaluate their own learning. The area they choose to study could be anything from math or history to car engines or comparative religions.

Self-directed learning, while good for all students, is particularly well suited to gifted students because of their internal drive to learn and their self-determination. The brighter the students, the more likely they will want to have a meaningful say in planning their own education.[17]

Self-directed learning is also good preparation for life after high school. I have often seen that the students who make a successful transition to the workload and expectations of college

> *I can remember having mad desires to learn how certain things worked, were put together, all from start to finish. Then, I could know and at last be satisfied.*
> (AAGC, 1978, p. 10)

education are those who own their learning and who are able to manage their time and their goals. They are the ones who know their own strengths and areas of struggle, who can ask for help when they need it, who can assess how well they are doing in order to make adjustments, and who are able to tolerate mundane work for the sake of greater goals. In short, they are self-directed learners. Because about 70% of adult learning is self-directed, these students are also preparing themselves for the world of work and family.[18]

Encouraging Self-Management

Because so much of modern teens' lives are dictated by traditions of school bells, bus schedules, sports practices, and other outside activities—the timing and management of which they have little or no control over—helping them learn and practice self-management skills at home is more important than ever. Here are some perspectives and habits that encourage the entire family to be more self-directed in learning and in life.

Take the Long View

Just like social-emotional development, self-management is a long-term process that is best approached in small steps and through the family environment. Remember that some gifted teens may take longer than usual for their executive functions to mature, through no fault of theirs or yours. The extra time needed for brain maturity may even result in higher executive functioning later on.[19] So while you might feel pressure or criticism from other parents or your own parents about whether or not your adolescent is learning to drive or getting an after-school job or showing other signs of adult independence, make those decisions based on your knowledge of your family, not what milestones others think your child should have reached by now.

Learning to drive is an excellent example. Many parents of highly gifted teens say that their children delayed getting a driver's license until age 17 or 18 or even later. The reasons that parents give are many—their teenager's perfectionism, an inability to trust intuition in difficult driving conditions, anxiety, or difficulty with concentration—but they all typically boil down to a combination of excitabilities and simply being "not quite ready" for driving, even if they are able to ace the written portion of the driving test.

Knowing that other families have this experience can be quite reassuring for parents who wonder if they are doing something wrong or if their teens are not developing normally. Just as a group of parents of young children laugh with recognition as they see how many others have to cut the tags off their children's clothes, simply knowing that they are not alone and that other parents of gifted teens also experience delayed milestones of adolescence brings a sigh of communal relief and a recognition that what is normal really is different for gifted families.

Make Expectations Clear

Parents can spend some time thinking about what expectations they have for their children and which ones are non-negotiable. For example, do you have expectations for what grades your children get? If so, exactly what are those expectations? A "B" average or better? A certain GPA? Do your parental expectations take into account the subjective nature of grading or the fact that perfection is not always possible? If your expectation is to "do your best," can you clarify what that means to you and what you look for?

Before you put together a final list, ask your children what expectations they have for themselves in areas such as grades, course selection, homework, extracurricular activities, part-time jobs, and so on. You can do this in a family discussion or by asking them to write down their ideas. Some families find that communicating by email is easier for these kinds of discussions, since it gives children time to process questions and provides a certain distance that encourages more objective thought. You might find that they have greater self-expectations than you realized and that you can step aside and work more on supporting their expectations and encouraging self-management skills rather than dictating from above.

Once you have your own list, see what you can cut out. Keep your list of non-negotiables as short as possible, but make them very clear. For example, instead of setting specific grades as expectations, you might have expectations for school attendance and homework, saying, for example, that you expect no unexcused absences and that homework is to be completed each night (or a specific period of study time) before your student does any computer games or phone calls or texting.

If your adolescent balks at items on your list, be open to compromise, but once you have discussed the issues and have made your decisions, stick by them. Be clear about how you will handle unmet expectations, and be sure your child understands any consequences. For example, especially if you are paying your teenager's cell phone bill, a reasonable consequence for habitual incompletion of homework because of time spent talking with or texting friends is to reduce the number of minutes or texts allowed on your family's phone plan, or possibly to have a "no cell phone" rule until homework or household chores are completed. You can even have a basket in a communal area where family members—parent included—put their cell phones when they want to concentrate on other work or when they want uninterrupted family time. If your child balks at your decision, have your response in mind and stick with it. For older teens, you might agree to pay for phone charges only if they keep up with schoolwork; otherwise, they have to earn the money to pay the fees themselves. This compromise allows you to enforce consequences while giving your teenager some responsibility and control.

When your children know what is non-negotiable from your point of view, they can better assess what self-direction they can use and what control they do have. This is why it is important to give them some areas in which they are in control of their time and space and choices, especially in later adolescence. In the areas where they do have flexibility, be sure to give them room for missteps as well as success. For instance, if you tell older teens that they can stay up as late as they want as long as they finish homework first, you shouldn't then complain when you see a light under their door at midnight. Likewise, if you agree that they can handle their own homework schedules as long as they maintain a specific GPA, you'll need to let them work through their own choice to do last-minute work and to deal with (and perhaps learn from) the anxiety it brings.

Notice and Legitimize Self-Direction

Parents can help teens see when and how they can be self-directed in their learning, regardless of external constraints. While there are many aspects of their education that neither you nor they can control, almost all situations have within them potential for some self-directed learning. Recognizing this potential can help adolescents feel more in control of their education and life.

For example, if a high school English class is not challenging enough, urge your child to think of practical ways that she can make the class more interesting. She can, of course, begin by talking to the teacher, but you can help her prepare by thinking of exactly what she will say. "This class is boring" will probably not get a good result. She will have a better chance for positive change if she explains that English is her strongest subject and she plans to pursue it further in college, so she was wondering if the teacher could give her some more complex writing assignments. If the teacher is unresponsive, your daughter still doesn't have to give up. You can help her find ways on her own to increase the level of challenge as a self-directed learner so that she is more likely to experience Flow in the class, maybe by doing additional critical reading about the literature that she is assigned or setting the goal of using new vocabulary in her essays or learning new ways to write introductions or conclusions. If you're near a junior college or university, it might be possible for your daughter to take or audit a more challenging course there. Or perhaps there is someone in the community who could act as a part-time mentor or tutor to work on more challenging assignments.

Families can also make time and room for children's interests, even if those interests have nothing to do with school or if they don't obviously lead to a career. When children learn because they want to learn, their skills of self-management are no less valuable than when they are doing assigned work. A teenager who teaches himself draw Japanese manga cartoons with proficiency, for example, is learning to set his own goals, find resources, work in a step-by-step fashion toward those goals, and assess his progress—all aspects of self-directed learning that can be applied in many other areas of his life. As parents, we can recognize and value these instances of self-directed learning in our children, however small they may be.

Focus on the Rewards of Overcoming Inertia

Trying not to procrastinate is like trying not to scratch an itch. The more we think about it, the harder it is to avoid. We all procrastinate at times. I chuckle at how often we parents complain about our children's procrastination and in the next breath rattle off all the items on our to-do list that are unfinished because we can't seem to motivate ourselves.

Rather than focusing simply on not procrastinating, we can help our children to know what rewards await them when they overcome feelings of inertia. Two ways do to this are to use Mihaly Csikszentmihalyi's theory of *Flow*, which we explored in Chapter 5, and to think about how we want to feel in the future.

Csikszentmihalyi reminds us that in addition to a drive to create, we humans are driven by a force that is just as strong, if not stronger—that is, inertia, the drive to do nothing and conserve our energy.[20] For tasks that are mundane but that are part of a larger goal, we can remind ourselves that the optimal experience of Flow requires that we first spend time gaining some necessary skills.

For example, a teenager who plays the piano might be tempted to skimp on practice time for finger exercises with the metronome because the task is difficult and tedious. If she can remember why she plays the piano to begin with, however, and recall times when she experienced Flow at the keyboard, she can tell herself that she will experience that Flow again once she gets over the hurdle of learning the new fingering skills. She might place on the piano, where she can see it, a piece that she will be able to play once she has mastered the new skills.

For everyday tasks that don't necessarily lead to bigger goals, we can allow ourselves to change our usual routines to make the job more enjoyable. For example, a student who needs to write a paper can challenge himself to make the task more fun by setting time limits (write non-stop for 10 minutes), or writing the paper backwards (writing the last paragraph first), or giving himself a reward for a certain number of words written. When he has to clean his room, he can put on his favorite music and dance while he cleans, or set a timer for five minutes to challenge himself to see how much he can finish in that time.

Another way to overcome inertia is to think of how we want to feel, not in the next five minutes, but tomorrow morning or in a week. When I assign papers to students, I often urge them to think about how they want to feel the morning the paper is due. Sometimes we actually take some time in class for them to close their eyes and imagine waking up in a week or two, knowing that their paper is ready and waiting: printed and proofread and stapled. I tell them to remember that feeling, and I ask them to draw up a detailed plan for themselves: when they want to have decided upon an idea, when they will have an outline or rough draft, when they will revise the paper, and so on. The combination of having the goal of a future feeling and a detailed plan for getting there helps many students—some for the first time—finish their work not only on time, but ahead of time.

Practice Breaking Big Goals into Small Steps

Many everyday family activities offer opportunities to learn and practice skills of planning and breaking large tasks into small ones. A few examples are planting a garden, training a puppy, or remodeling a bedroom. By including the whole family—even young children—in the planning process for these long-term activities, parents can offer practice in setting goals and schedules and delegating tasks.

Offer many options for how teens plan their time and manage their space. Depending on your family budget, you might want to take a trip to the local office supply store to look at weekly planners, white boards, chalkboards, plastic organizing bins, colorful folders, and other ways to keep spaces organized. Our son has in his room a large white board with colored markers. He has used the white board in many ways to help him stay organized, sometimes by listing to-do items and prioritizing them by color, other times writing the number of minutes he plans to spend on a specific task or activity. Instead of lists, some people prefer using creative thinking organizers such as Tony Buzan's Mind Mapping technique (see the recommended resources at the end of Chapter 5), or your teen might need to doodle and draw in order to plan most effectively, so a sketchbook might work better as a planner than a calendar format.

Depending on the age of your children and your relationship with them, you might be able to talk about these self-management techniques directly. For older teens who may be resistant to overt advice, you can begin by being more open about your own planning strategies and the small steps you make toward goals, knowing that they are watching, even if they don't say anything. Leave to-do lists lying on the kitchen table. Ask your teen to remind you about tasks that you have set for yourself, as a favor to you. Reward yourself for small accomplishments toward your goals in ways that involve the whole family, such as going out for dinner or ice cream, or going to a movie or renting a DVD. And encourage your teens to reward themselves for small accomplishments as well as large ones.

Expect Asynchronous Development as Normal

Don't mistake intellectual capacity for maturity of judgment, nor emotional excitability for emotional maturity. While it might seem odd that a 16-year-old can learn differential calculus or discuss Keynesian economics but fail a driving test because of impulsivity and poor judgment or anxiety, such asynchrony is normal for many gifted adolescents. Likewise, the depth of feeling that comes with emotional excitability does not necessarily translate into being able to understand or manage those feelings, nor does it mean that gifted teens might not react to strong feelings in inappropriate ways, such as pouting or yelling.

Adults can resist the temptation to use this asynchronous development against teens, even in well-meaning attempts to change their behavior. It simply won't work to say, "You're so smart; if you'd just apply yourself, you could pass that driving test and control your nerves," or, "I wish you'd act gifted." Frontal lobe maturity cannot be rushed, and the asynchronous development is not the adolescent's fault. What gifted teens need most in these situations is nurturing guidance and reassurance that their different developmental levels are normal and that, in time, they will have more control over their thoughts, emotions, and actions.

At the same time, keep in mind that gifted children *can* also have learning differences and personality disorders such as Attention Deficit Disorder (ADD), autism, dyslexia, and Oppositional Defiant Disorder (ODD). Children who are "gifted and" are sometimes called *twice-exceptional* students because they have exceptional needs in more than one area. Discerning whether learning difficulties are due to "normal" asynchronous development or another condition that could be improved through professional guidance and specialized understanding is not always easy. Gifted children are sometimes misdiagnosed with disorders, in part because diagnostic categories seldom take into consideration the differences of giftedness.[21] Parents who want to learn more about twice-exceptional learners can read *Misdiagnosis and Dual Diagnoses of Gifted Children and Adults: ADHD, Bipolar, OCD, Asperger's, Depression, and Other Disorders*, written by James Webb and five other experts in the field of gifted education and psychology (see the resources at the end of Chapter 3), as well as the *2e: Twice-Exceptional Newsletter* (http://2enewsletter.com).

Show, Don't Tell

Do your best not to nag or scold. I know, this one is hard! When you see your son—yet again—leave papers at home that he needed for school, resist the urge to remind him how often this has happened in the past. He probably feels bad enough on his own, and parental pushing and prodding will only make him focus on your relationship rather than prompt him to improve self-management skills.

Develop and learn to trust your inner voice and your knowledge of your child. Ask yourself when you think it is okay to step in to help, and when you should step back and allow your child to learn from experience, and then, once you have decided, let your choices and actions speak for themselves. This line is different for every child and parent, so don't feel that you need to do what other parents do. Whatever you decide, however, stick to your plan without unnecessary explaining or cajoling.

For example, your neighbor might expect her daughter to be responsible for arranging her own transportation to school and other events, and she might not want to be involved at all in her child's homework or study schedule. Those practices might work just fine for her family, but you don't need to feel that you are unnecessarily rescuing your daughter if you decide to drive her to school or support her in organizing her homework, especially if you see that your daughter is lagging in executive functions. Likewise, if you make a decision that your son needs to experience the natural consequences of forgetting his math book at home rather than your bringing it to him at school, learn to trust your knowledge and instincts as a parent rather than be swayed by your own mother, who tells you that are being too hard on him and that "boys are just forgetful."

Also, be aware of how you model self-management in your work and family life. Children learn much more from what they see us do than what we try to tell them. This doesn't mean that we have to be perfectly organized and working toward goals every minute of the day. In fact, we would do well to be honest with ourselves and our children about the compromises that we make and the ways in which we meet and don't meet the expectations that we have for ourselves. The important thing is to offer a real, human example for our children of someone who continues to learn new skills of self-direction and self-management.

Accommodate Intellectual Needs

Use creativity to construct environments that accommodate asynchronous development. A challenge unique to many gifted teens is that they are ready for college-level work before they are necessarily ready for the life of a college student. Deirdre Lovecky explains:

> They simply have not had the life experience to feel or be safe enough to live away from home, nor to make the choices that young adults commonly have to make in college. Some are happy to live at home if that can be arranged; others are chafing at the structure of home. They want nothing more than to leave and be their own persons at an age when they are really not prepared to meet the challenges of self-directed work, or the personal responsibility of day to day living needs.[22]

Parents in this situation can use creative thinking skills to find solutions that will meet their teens' intellectual needs without expecting too much from them in terms of social-emotional development or self-management. Talent search programs open the door to high-level learning opportunities without requiring students to graduate from high school early. Adult community classes, both formal and informal, are often open to teens who are ready for higher level learning. Self-motivated teens can also take advantage of technology and the "open courseware" movement in higher education to teach themselves college-level subjects and skills that they otherwise couldn't afford or have access to. Open courseware refers to college lectures, notes, and other materials made available for free on the Internet (see the recommended resources at the end of this chapter).

If you live in a city with local community colleges or universities, your teenager might be able to take concurrent college and high school classes, known as *dual enrollment*. Other parents find that early high school graduation and either part- or full-time college attendance as a commuter student is a good alternative. Still others homeschool, giving their adolescents more freedom to learn at appropriate levels or specialization.

Of course, a few highly gifted teenagers *are* ready to go to college early and live on campus with no ill effects. These young people tend to be very goal-oriented and are unusually independent for their age. See the resources at the end of the next chapter for how to find residential college programs that are receptive to young students.

Give the Gift of Courage

Finally, we can give young people a gift that we as their parents are best prepared to offer: the permission and courage to live their own lives. James Webb writes of the "imbalance" that occurs when gifted people lack courage:

> *These creative persons care deeply about others and about their impact on the world, and long to have a meaningful place in it. However, creative action is restricted or blocked because of shyness, fear, or anxiety, or because of a depressing and paralyzing awareness of how limited one person's impact on the world typically is.*[23]

While we can't change whether our children are naturally shy or anxious, we can influence how they view those traits in themselves. We can also offer our home as a safe place to learn and practice self-determination, a place where everyone *does* have an impact and where everyone's drive is valued and nurtured, even when it makes life more complicated or goes against our own preferences and tastes.

When your teenage son wants to take theater instead of sign up for football, even though you, as his father, always dreamed of his following in your footsteps as a varsity all-star, you can recognize your son's self-determination rather than view his preference as rejection of you, and give him room and permission

> *My parents let me do things I want to do.... I am free and independent. They talk to me like an adult; they trust me, and I respect them. The only differences we have had are those of degree; they sometimes harped too much on achievement. They wanted awards; not me. I was indifferent.* (AAGC, 1978, p. 41)

to choose his own path in life. When your daughter is determined to go to law school, even though you yourself are uncomfortable with high achievement because of your own upbringing, you can be grateful that she has the drive to follow her dreams, and you can support her every step of the way. When your child registers as a Republican while you are a lifelong Democrat (or vice versa), you will give an invaluable gift by accepting her choice, even if you strongly disagree with it.

When we are open to the possibilities, every day offers the chance to give our children this gift of courage and the permission to own and direct their own lives—and that's not to say that it will always be our first inclination or that it will be easy.

Recommended Further Reading and Resources

Response to Intervention and the Autonomous Learner Model: A Complete Approach for the Gifted and Talented
By George Betts & Robin J. Carey
ALP Publishing, 2009
This detailed and useful guide for helping students to become more self-directed learners includes many ideas for self-discovery, career exploration, and planning for the future. You can download the free article "The Autonomous Learning Model for High School Programming" by George Betts from the publisher's website at www.alpspublishing.com/alm.html.

Guerrilla Learning: How to Give Your Kids a Real Education With or Without School
By Grace Llewellyn & Amy Silver
Wiley, 2001
This reader-friendly book offers encouragement and ideas for helping children—whether homeschooled or in school—to be more self-directed learners.

Open Courseware
The Universities and websites below offer free courseware that motivated students can use to learn everything from architecture to zoology.

- Academic Earth
  http://academicearth.org

- Massachusetts Institute of Technology (MIT) OpenCourseWare
  http://ocw.mit.edu/OcwWeb

- The Open University
  http://openlearn.open.ac.uk

- University of California, Berkeley Webcast
  http://webcast.berkeley.edu

- YouTube EDU
  www.youtube.com/education

Classes, Camps, and Conferences for Intense Learners

The following are just a few of the many opportunities across the nation where children and teens can learn with intensity in the company of like-minded peers.

- Concordia Language Villages (Minnesota)
  www.concordialanguagevillages.org

  World language immersion and new cultural experiences in a summer camp

- Cybercamps
  www.giantcampus.com/cybercamps

  Technology, digital media, and gaming camps throughout the country

- Duke University Youth Programs (North Carolina)
  www.learnmore.duke.edu/youth

  Summer academic enrichment in a variety of areas

- Interlochen Arts Camp (Michigan)
  http://camp.interlochen.org

  Summer programs for creative writing, dance, general arts, motion picture arts, music theatre arts, and visual arts

- Johns Hopkins Center for Talented Youth (Maryland)
  http://cty.jhu.edu

  Online classes, summer programs, and school-year courses

- Northwestern University Center for Talent Development (Illinois)
  www.ctd.northwestern.edu

  Summer, Saturday, and online programs

- SENG Conference Teen Programs"
  www.sengifted.org/conference_about.shtml

  A program for teens of parents who attend the SENG (Supporting Emotional Needs of the Gifted) conference

- THINK Summer Institute (Nevada)
  www.davidsongifted.org/think

  An intense, three-week summer program for exceptionally and profoundly gifted youth

- University of Northern Colorado Summer Enrichment Program
  www.unco.edu/cebs/sep

  A summer residential program for gifted, talented, and creative youth

Chapter 7

Multipotentiality:
When Teens Are Good at Many Things

*Helping adolescents and young adults find the sources of work
and love that rekindle the passions of the preschool years are the
tasks educators, parents, therapists, and young people themselves
are faced with. Only through finding satisfying life's work and
satisfying relationships can the gifted young person grow into
adulthood.*

~ Deirdre Lovecky[1]

Multipotentiality is a term used to refer to having the potential to
succeed in many areas. Teens with multipotentiality do well in
several subject areas and are interested and involved in many different
activities—academics, sports, community service, leadership, fine arts.
Others may have a more focused interested—music, for example—but
within that interest have a variety of skills, such as the ability to perform,
compose, conduct, grasp music theory, and give lessons.

Multipotentiality can be a great asset. Not only does it give young
people many options for study and future careers, it also can be the
source of a number of fulfilling hobbies. People with multipotentiality
are also often able to synthesize ideas from different subject areas to
create new knowledge and offer comprehensive theories. Within a
company, a worker with multipotentiality has the ability to work across
different departments or move to a new department. Having more
options and skills also allows adults to switch gears mid-career and move
to an entirely new career, whether by choice or necessity.

However, for some of the same reasons, multipotentiality can also be a problem, especially for adolescents. How does a girl who knows she can succeed as an engineer, a writer, and a teacher make a decision about her future without feeling as if she is shutting the door on other possibilities that excite her? How does she prioritize her choices when all of her aptitudes seem equally high? Or how does a young boy choose between preparation for law school and an internship in the arts, both of which appeal to him and each of which seems to preclude the other?

Another challenge for young people with many interests and skills is that they spread themselves too thin in an effort to do it all, sacrificing both sleep and even the time necessary to do any of their activities to the best of their abilities. As James Webb explains, they may realize early and painfully that they simply cannot do all that they want to do:

> *Although they try to cram 27 hours worth of living into a 24-hour day, there simply isn't enough time to develop all of the talents and interests that they may have. They have to make choices, but the choices among so many possibilities feel unfair because they seem arbitrary; there is no "ultimately right" choice. Choosing a college major or avocation is difficult when one is trying to make a decision between passion and talent in areas as diverse as violin, genetics, theoretical mathematics, and international relations. How can one be all that one can be? In truth, one cannot be all that one "could" be in every area.[2]*

This frustration can continue past adolescence, as adults with multipotentiality may find themselves drifting from job to job, unable to settle in any spot long enough to know if it would satisfy over the long term, feeling that their lives and careers are a hodge-podge of failed attempts. Dabbling in many and varied interest areas without focusing on one to become proficient or expert in can lead to dissatisfaction with what "might have been."

Finding Passions and Making Choices

A study published in the *Journal of Counseling Psychology* suggests that multipotentiality may not be not as problematic nor even as prevalent as we have been led to believe, or at least that we may want to think about multipotentiality differently. According to the study's authors, the "illusion" that many gifted students are "equally competent at everything" comes from their ability to do well in a variety of academic subjects and their involvement in a variety of in-school and after-school activities. However, such measures create an artificial ceiling that doesn't allow us to see a student's relative strengths.[3]

Think of a top high school student who gets A's in English, math, and science classes, is on the varsity basketball team, edits the school newspaper, and is president of the student council. She makes everything look effortless, and perhaps because of psychomotor intensity, she likes to keep busy, so she gets involved in many activities. As she begins to think about college and career choices, she panics, unsure of how to prioritize her many strengths and interests. She wants to do it all!

Rather than indicate that this student is equally good at everything, this picture might instead be telling us that she is not being challenged at a level to show her relative passions and aptitudes. Perhaps she would continue to thrive and be engaged in college-level math but find college-level literature more frustrating and less interesting. Or, alternatively, she might excel as a newspaper intern but find that her interest in math wanes at higher levels.

Our hypothetical student who easily aces high school chemistry, which takes up an hour or less of her day, might be tempted to think that being a chemist is what she "should" do. However, she might find that a full-time job in a lab doesn't suit her temperament at all, and she might find her true passion, or what Ken Robinson calls her *Element*, by working with the leadership skills that she honed as student council president, instead of the more solitary nature of scientific study.[4]

As we learned in Chapter 2, Robinson defines the *Element* as "the meeting point between natural aptitude and personal passion." When people find their Element—whether it is their full-time job, hobby, or approach to life in general—"they connect with something fundamental to their sense of identity, purpose, and well-being."[5] Mihaly Csikszentmihalyi would refer to this connection as *Flow*. The authors of the *Journal of Counseling Psychology* article describe it as "optimal adjustment"—a match between personal abilities, personal preferences, and requirements and rewards from the workplace environment.[6]

Finding our niche in life is a personal journey, one that has no template or set of instructions. We can experience the joy that being in our Element can bring in nearly any area—academic subjects, interpersonal communication, physical activity, creative invention, fine arts—as long as we find that meeting point of what we are good at and what we love.

Whether your children have many interests or a few, multiple areas of potential or a single, unwavering talent, as a parent, you are uniquely suited to encouraging them to find their Element. Parents know their children inside and out and can watch for areas in which their children not only do well, but become one with their study or activity. We can also urge young people to think about their college and career choices in terms of how rewarding they would find the environment of long-term study or work in those areas.[7]

> *I have always been interested in medicine and, through a career interest form I filled out in school, I was contacted by a local hospital to take part in a program sponsored by a local Explorers Post. We had meetings once a week at the hospital, where we would hear a wide variety of medical specialists. During the rest of the week we would set up times when we would work in different areas of the hospital such as radiology, physical therapy, emergency room, etc. This was a very good experience for me, since it allowed me to get a...feel [for] different health and medical fields.* (AAGC, 1978, pp. 103-4)

If your child will be a first-generation college student, learning the skills and attitudes necessary to bridge the gap between school achievement and a successful career is especially important, since the experience is a new one for your family and you don't have your own college experience to draw upon. Without guidance as to what careers are within reach and how to get there from here, first-generation college students often narrow their choices to jobs that are upwardly mobile rather than careers that have the potential to be "deeply, intrinsically meaningful."[8]

Parents can encourage students to investigate and be exposed to the real-world environment of areas that they are interested in through either formal or informal mentorships. Some high schools offer mentorship or intern programs with local professionals and businesses. These programs are typically taken for high school credit, and they offer valuable insights into the world of work and professional relationships. If no such program exists where you live, you can ask family members or friends to serve as informal mentors for teenagers. The parents of one young woman I know who was interested in animal science found for their daughter a local dog breeder who was willing to be a mentor for a few hours a week. Parents who are interested in learning more about or creating mentoring possibilities can read *Mentorship: The Essential Guide for Schools and Business*, by Jill M. Reilly.

Helping Teens Find Their Niche

To help teens consider majors and careers that are possible good fits, parents can offer opportunities to explore a wide variety of subject areas and activities. This is particularly important for children who are introverts. Although the advantage of introversion for gifted teens is that they are less tempted to overextend themselves and their schedules, parents can still look for possible classes, groups, camps, and mentorships, whether through talent search programs, community groups, or online resources. Leave the choice of how involved to be up to the child, but make available many options, both in areas of strength and in areas previously unexplored.

Remind young people that they have a lifetime to explore their many skills, interests, and passions. If they are not sure at age 16 or 18 of what they want to do for the rest of their lives, the verdict is not "Do not pass go, do not collect $200." Likewise, even if they are clear about their future career, they should be open to the possibility that they might eventually change their minds and paths. The Bureau of Labor Statistics estimates that in the 30 years after high school, adults hold an average of 10 different jobs.[9] Given the fast pace of changing technology, the careers our children eventually enter might not even be invented yet, much less have majors to lead them there! All of this reminds us that finding one's Element or Flow should not be a stressful endeavor or yet another high-stakes pursuit. Rather, it is a lifetime journey without a single destination, one that has many unplanned side trips and restful stops along the way.

To live a life full of Flow, we need not necessarily make our passion area a career. My brother is a perfect example. A photography major in college, he decided, as an adult with a family, to photograph in his free time as a hobby, at least for now while his son is young, and to work in a job that gives him good benefits, time to enjoy fatherhood, and the freedom to race mountain bikes and snowboard, which are activities he loves. Eventually he may find a way to make a living with his photography, but for now, he continues to hone his skills and indulge his passion without having to work full-time in a studio, something he probably would not enjoy as much as freelance work.

For students who have a laser-like focus in a single area, in the words of E. Paul Torrance, who is often referred to as the Father of Creativity, "Don't waste a lot of expensive, unproductive energy trying to be well-rounded." Multipotentiality is not a criterion for giftedness. Many of the students I teach at an engineering college have known since before they can remember that they want to build things when they grow up. They bring their LEGO blocks to college, daydream about new bridge designs, and read *Popular Mechanics* for fun. Once when I asked members of the class to draw self-portraits as part of an art appreciation lesson, one of them drew his own head as an electrical circuit. He assured me that it was a working electrical circuit, and I took his word for it. These engineering students usually have little interest in creative writing or fiction.

Although I enjoy exposing them to literature and other aspects of the humanities—and some find that they are more interested in those areas than they had thought—most of my students have already found their passion, their Element, and are ready and eager to get started. Is there a problem when a student does not on his own accord read fiction? Certainly not. I know many adults who don't read fiction. They prefer nonfiction: newspapers, magazines, biographies, historical accounts, or science books. Reading some fiction while young is a good thing simply because it offers exposure to a rich literary world. However, exposure to literature does not guarantee a love for literature. I have come to respect the fact that my engineering students have a love for numbers and equations and formulas in the same way that I have a love for words and stories and symbolism.

Keep in mind that an area of passion might not necessarily be in our greatest area of natural ability. Your child might whip off an expertly written essay without much effort but not be the least bit interested in a writing career, instead wanting to be a computer programmer, even though this field requires more conscious study and effort on her part because it doesn't come as naturally. This point is particularly important to remember when a child shows an early and unusual ability in an area that requires intensive training, such as music or math. While adults might worry that such talent not be "wasted," at the same time, they can be watchful for signs that the child's interests actually lie elsewhere. Ken Robinson also reminds us that our Element can be a specific subset of an activity, such as jazz music instead of classical, or spatial math instead of statistics—another argument for exposing our children to a wide range of knowledge and types of jobs.

Finally, don't be swayed by pressure to narrow choices too early. In generations past, college was a time of broad study and exploration. Today, high school students are asked not just about where they plan to go to college, but what their major(s) will be, and they are urged to choose "practical" majors and seek "career-building" internships before they have a chance to figure out who they are or what they would enjoy doing. An article in *Duke Gifted Letter* reminds us:

> *Gifted teens can experience enormous stress while trying to resolve personal identity issues, satisfy their psychological needs, and overcome their anxieties about leaving home and making ends meet. The internal and external pressures to pursue specialized academic training that will lead to a prestigious occupation can be damaging, especially for adolescents who are talented in areas other than traditional academic.*[10]

To lessen this stress, you can share with your children examples from your own life of how you continue to discover new passions or new aspects of old passions. Parents can also encourage and value skills of personal and interpersonal communication, flexible decision making, managing change, and lifelong learning.

My parents were most helpful to me by serving as excellent role models, especially my mother, who has expanded her learning by holding many different kinds of jobs. She has been everything from an English major to a chemist to the director of an acting troupe in post-war Germany to a medical librarian to an economics librarian to the head of a data bank. And each time she has changed jobs, she has jumped into a field she knew very little about. (AAGC, 1978, pp. 51-2)

Recommended Further Reading

Cool Colleges: For the Hyper-Intelligent, Self-Directed, Late Blooming, and Just Plain Different
By Donald Asher
Ten Speed Press, 2007
This fun book will open your eyes to a wide variety of college options, from the Ivy League to Great Books programs, engineering schools to maritime colleges.

College Planning for Gifted Students: Choosing and Getting into the Right College
By Sandra L. Berger
Prufrock Press, 3rd edition, 2006
Sandra Berger's comprehensive book gives clear guidelines for college planning, including a list of early college entrance programs, a schedule of tasks for the junior year, advice for choosing between and taking SAT, ACT, and AP exams, and information about how to handle college applications. See the publisher's website for an interview with the author and to read a sample chapter: www.prufrock.com.

The New Global Student: Skip the SAT, Save Thousands on Tuition, and Get a Truly International Education
By Maya Frost
Crown/Three Rivers Press, 2009
If you or your child has ever wondered if it would be possible to sidestep altogether the artificial constraints of a traditional college prep high school education—if only in your attitude—this book is a must-read. Maya Frost describes today's new "bold student" as artful, advanced, atypical, and adventurous, and she writes that "they key to success" for these students "is a sense of *being fully involved in their own education*" (author's emphasis). Learn more and read a sample chapter on the author's website at www.mayafrost.com/new-global-student-book.htm.

Conquering the SAT: How Parents Can Help Teens Overcome the Pressure and Succeed
By Ned Johnson & Emily Warner Eskelsen
Palgrave Macmillan, 2006
This well-written book offers a refreshing and practical insight on how parents can be on their children's side and keep matters in perspective during SAT preparation.

"College Planning for Gifted and Talented Youth"

By Barbara Kerr
Available on the National Association for Gifted Children (NAGC) website: www.nagc.org/index.aspx?id=202
In this thoughtful article, Barbara Kerr, author of *Smart Girls* and co-author of *Smart Boys*, discusses college and career planning both for students with multipotentiality and for students whose career interests are already focused. Her suggestions are broken down for elementary, junior high, high school, and college levels. She also includes a section for minorities and women.

Uniquely Gifted: Especially for Parents: College

By Meredith Warshaw
www.uniquelygifted.org/especially_for_parents.htm#_College
Meredith Warshaw's well-researched and valuable website for twice-exceptional students offers links to several resources about college preparation and admissions for gifted students who also have learning differences.

Chapter 8

The Gifted Parent

When I give talks to homeschooling or other groups, introducing them to the idea of intensity and how giftedness affects their children and families, the room is always filled with a nearly palpable energy. By the end of the talk, someone inevitably mentions that the excitability and drive and other traits that we have been discussing describe not only her children, but herself or her partner or her parents. Heads around the person then begin to nod and, more often than not, someone begins to cry as he or she recalls the experience of being a gifted adult:

> *To feel like an outsider, to constantly pressure yourself to hold back your gifts in order to fit in or avoid disapproval, to erroneously believe that you are overly sensitive, compulsively perfectionistic, and blindly driven, to live without knowing the basic truths about the core of your being....*[1]

Many adults are relieved to understand their children better when they learn about intensity and giftedness, but they are reluctant to think of themselves as gifted. As we discussed in Chapter 2, there is really no need for anyone to apply any label to themselves if they don't want to. What is important, however, is for parents to know, accept, and like themselves for who they are. Giftedness helps to describe people who have a complex combination of high ability in one or more areas, intensity, excitability, drive, creativity, and sensibility. If you have one or more of these traits, whether you decide to think of yourself as gifted is less important than your realizing that the gifted difference does apply to you and affects your experience, relationships, and sense of self.

> [My parents] hindered me at times by often expecting too much of me. By being perfectionists, my parents made me feel inadequate and frustrated if I was not constantly performing at my best. (AAGC, 1978, p. 49)

Unless and until intense parents come to terms with their own gifted traits, they inevitably see their children's needs through the lens of their own feelings of being misunderstood. Far from being a selfish act, learning to know and accept yourself as you are is perhaps the greatest gift you can give your family.

Adult Excitabilities and Development

Dabrowski's concept of overexcitabilities and his larger theory of positive disintegration apply to adults as well as children. Although we already discussed overexcitabilities in Chapter 3, let's review Dabrowski's five areas of overexcitability (OE):[2]

- *Intellectual OE*: has abilities of analysis and synthesis, asks probing questions, loves learning for its own sake

- *Emotional OE*: is sensitive, experiences emotions intensely, is empathic toward others, takes things to heart

- *Imaginational OE*: is a daydreamer, has a rich fantasy life, is creative

- *Psychomotor OE*: has high energy, is curious, has difficulty sitting still, needs constant change of scenery, is generally restless

- *Sensual OE*: is highly sensitive to sensory perceptions such as sights, sounds, smells, tastes, and tactile stimulation

Remember that these overexcitabilities are not meant to be tests of giftedness, but they do help many gifted people understand their intensities better and accept their internal differences. Overexcitabilities are part of Dabrowski's theory of positive disintegration. According to Dabrowski, OEs—especially the "Big Three" of intellectual, imagination, and emotional—carry the potential for higher personal development because they are like an itch that must be scratched. People with OEs "are likely to experience surprise and puzzlement at events in their daily lives," and when this puzzlement is combined with self-reflection and the pain of realizing that we want to be in some way better than we currently are, the potential for personal growth arises.[3]

In Dabrowski's theory of positive disintegration, described earlier, the essence is that the negative disintegration of some part of the self—"falling apart"—leads to a number of choices and possible outcomes. We might get stuck in the disintegration, sinking into long-term depression or other mental difficulties. We might decide to go back to our old way of living and thinking because it is easier than the pain of disintegration. Or we might work through the disintegration, making it positive by continuing on a lifelong journey of growth into better versions of our self. As James Webb explains:

> *Conformity can be comforting; being an individual, particularly if one is challenging traditions, is often uncomfortable. Dabrowski clearly believed that one cannot evolve into a fully developed and authentic person without developing an individualistic, unique, and conscious inner core of beliefs and values. He also understood that this road was arduous and fraught with discomfort and pain.*[4]

The theory of positive disintegration is particularly useful for gifted individuals at midlife, when old ways of thinking and living may no longer serve them well. Mary Elaine Jacobsen tells us in her book *The Gifted Adult* that middle age is often when gifted adults experience a crisis of identity pertaining to the gifted differences of intensity, complexity, and drive.[5]

Big Three Gifted Differences: Intensity, Complexity, and Drive

By now, the gifted traits of intensity, complexity, and drive should be familiar. Jacobsen argues that the goal for adults is to recognize, understand, and finally manage these traits so that they are neither collapsed nor exaggerated. For example, she lists verbal agility as a part of intensity. An adult with a balanced management of verbal agility can use these strengths:[6]

- Engaging conversationalist
- Comfortable with intense discussion
- Colorful storyteller
- Sincere spokesperson
- Persuasive
- Articulate
- Stimulating

On the other hand, collapsed verbal agility looks like this:

- Dodges controversy
- Steers toward popular opinion
- Dull and unimaginative speech
- Can't hold the floor
- Vague
- Spineless fence-straddler
- Substitutes mindless banter for in-depth conversation

And exaggerated verbal agility shows itself as follows:

- Intractable opinions
- Dominates conversations
- Embellishes the truth
- Poses embarrassing questions
- Coercive
- Lectures and corrects others
- Caustic, using words as weapons

The Big Three gifted differences become mismanaged, collapsed, or exaggerated over time because adults haven't been taught to understand them or use them. The good news is that the years of parenting during midlife are a good time for self-reflection, revision of our own self-understanding, and a conscious movement toward a revised set of thoughts and behaviors.

Go back to Annemarie Roeper's list of gifted traits in Chapter 2. This time, think about them not as they pertain to your children, but how well they fit your own experience or that of your partner. If you are beginning to see the gifted difference in yourself, try using some of the resources at the end of the chapter to learn about what makes you tick.

Parenting with Intensity: The Perils of High Potential

When children have obvious or valued talents, high levels of intellectual aptitude, or are "globally gifted" in the sense that they seem able to be very accomplished at everything they try, we parents are naturally tempted to project into their future the fruition of their potential. Even if we don't daydream about our child's accepting the Nobel Peace Prize or Pulitzer, friends and teachers will no doubt offer plenty of free advice about how not to squander our child's abilities. The authors of *Conquering the SAT: How Parents Can Help Teens Overcome the Pressure and Succeed* explain how, in wanting to do the best for our children, we might convince ourselves that they really are too young to understand their own potential, and it is our job not just to nurture it, but to fulfill it for them:

> *As parents, we all want the best for our children. We want our children to be successful. We may even feel that we want to give them success. There is, however, a twist: the goal of all parents should be to develop within their children the attributes and skills they need in order to make themselves successful. It is perilously easy to conflate that with just making their kids successful.[7]*

We can't fool ourselves about the temptation to cross that fine line between offering healthy support and being able to step back as necessary, on the one hand, and over-managing, over-controlling, and over-scheduling on the other. There is no shame in admitting, if only to ourselves, that we aren't always sure if we are pushing too hard or not supporting enough. This fine line is especially hard to walk for parents of gifted children for several reasons, including our children's sensitivities, wanting to repair our own past life experiences, reluctance to be in charge, our propensity for intense parenting, and the urge to perfect.

Our Children's Sensitivities

Some (but certainly not all) gifted children are very good at figuring out what we want from them and doing whatever they can to please us. They pick up on the slightest change in our tone, expression, or choice of words. They can tell the difference between when we are saying something we really mean and when our words say one thing but our real message is something else. Gifted, sensitive, and intuitive children can internalize unspoken parental expectations about levels of achievement, grades, even future choices of college or career to the point that they are no longer even aware that these goals are their parents' goals and not their own. Often the parents do not realize what has happened and are convinced that their children have chosen these goals for themselves. Only much later, when the child is a young adult and on his own, does a crisis of identity occur as he begins the process of detangling who he is and what he wants from the pull to please his parents.

Wanting to Fix Our Own Past

Because giftedness often is a family trait, many parents of smart, talented children relive a lot of frustration from their own childhoods as they learn more about the experience of being gifted. They might be tempted, with the best of intentions, to "fix" everything for their children that went wrong with their own education and early childhood experiences. Many adults of my generation feel that they were more or less left to their own devices in terms of pursuing their dreams or embracing the power of their potential, at least in comparison with today's highly involved parents. If you harbor resentments from your early years about what your parents did or didn't do for you, you might go far out of your way to offer your own children every opportunity that you were denied and to be the involved parent that you wish your parents had been.

Reluctance to Be in Charge

From a very young age, gifted children can be excellent companions. Their curiosity is infectious. Their company allows adults to relive the joys of childhood. Their conversations are not only lively, but also interesting and often informative. They can be very persuasive and are masters of debate before they can ride a bike or, in some cases, even before they are potty trained.

By the time these verbally gifted children reach adolescence, parents can easily find themselves in a pattern of endless argument. Not wanting to resort to using "because I said so" as a way to resolve every dispute, parents might lack other ways to influence and guide their children when necessary for safety or health. Some parents are reluctant to be in charge, and it can be especially difficult if the parents want to suddenly start taking charge when a youngster reaches the teen years.

Knowing the value of democratic rather than "I told you so" parenting, many parents today balk at the idea of controlling their children in an authoritarian way. But being in charge of others is different from being in control. We can be in control of *ourselves*, but we cannot control how others think or feel or even how they act (although we can enforce consequences for actions). However, we still need to be in charge. Intelligence is not the same as wisdom or life experience.

Being in charge means owning our responsibility. Thinking of our children as being in our charge means that we set certain boundaries for them until they can do so for themselves. We keep them safe while they are in our care because they need someone to consider the dangers that they cannot see or imagine. Because of the asynchronous development of gifted children and their lagging judgment compared to their intellectual abilities, parents sometimes have to draw those boundaries firmly and enforce guidelines of behavior with clear consequences.

For example, suppose your high school freshman has been invited through online contacts to a university gaming group. You have seen him struggle to find friends with similar interests, and you are tempted to allow him to attend an all-night gaming marathon at a college dorm. He has argued (or perhaps pouted) his case for weeks, maintaining that he is responsible and can take care of himself, and that he has given you no reason not to trust him. While you cannot bear to see his disappointment or anger, you have major reservations. You do not know the other gamers. Your son would be the only high school student there, and he is a young high school student. You have no idea how many of the other gamers are of drinking age or how the gaming sessions are conducted.

Being in charge in this kind of situation probably means telling your son that he cannot attend the event, regardless of his reaction to your decision or how the decision makes you feel as you enforce it. Once you make your decision, it is okay to let your son know that the time for debate is finished. You do not have a responsibility to rebut his every point or to apologize for being firm. You are in charge of his safety, but you are not in control of his reactions or feelings.

This kind of boundary setting is more difficult for some parents than for others, but it will be necessary at some point. If you know that being in charge will be difficult, find other adult support for your decisions—a partner, family member, or friend—who can remind you of why you are making the hard but right choice. Especially if your child resists your decision and reacts with predicted intensity, remind yourself that this, too, shall pass and that you are doing what is necessary to ensure your child's health, safety, and continued growth. The problem is that reactionary parenting can easily overlook the needs of the child in front of us—a child who is his or her own person with unique needs and circumstances.

As another example, suppose you have decided that you want your teenager to wait an extra year to take driver's education classes because, at the moment, she is unpredictably emotional and easily distracted, more so than is typical for her age. She tries to argue her case. She pouts. She says that you are unfair and don't trust her. She refuses to talk to you for days. In this kind of situation, when you are making a decision based on what is in your child's best interest for health and safety, you will need the courage mentioned in Chapter 1 to stick to your resolve. Also, you can be careful to be firm without blaming your daughter for asynchronous development that she cannot control. None of this is easy, especially if we did not have examples from our own childhoods of parents who were good boundary setters. Having a friend or family member who supports your decision can help you to stay focused on *why* you have made this choice and to remind you that, in the long run, it doesn't matter whether your daughter gets a driver's license at age 17 instead of 16.

Intense Parenting and the Urge to Perfect[8]

Intensity and a perfectionistic nature do not disappear with age. Gifted adults—regardless of whether they identify themselves as gifted—often bring to everything they do a high level of passion and intensity, and this includes their parenting. For example, your child might express in passing an interest in learning to play the violin. Your natural excitement about something new and challenging kicks in, and before long you have read nine articles about finding the best violin teacher, visited three local music stores to look at different instruments, and reorganized a room in your house for your child to use as a practice studio—all before your child has played the first note on the violin. You congratulate yourself for being attuned to your child's desires and needs. But is this level of involvement simply a way of providing opportunity and support? Or is it a sign that you might need to direct that energy and passion toward something that *you* want to do, something less focused on molding your child's experience? Our own urge to perfect can shine its light directly on our children so as to try to make everything about their childhood and their education not only good, but perfect, whatever the cost.

If we are honest, most of us will recognize ourselves in at least some of the above descriptions. This does not mean that we are bad parents! In fact, I would argue that the problem starts when we ignore our ambivalence about how to raise and educate our children, when we rush blindly ahead without self-reflection, and when we trust too much in the advice of others without consulting and learning to trust ourselves.

Here are some ways to avoid the temptation to "make our kids successful" and instead give them the tools they need to create their own success:

- Remind yourself that giftedness is not measured by external success or awards. Your children's intensity, sensitivity, and intelligence will not go away if they are not at the top of their class, don't get the lead in the play, or choose to go to a small local college instead of to Oxford. "Making them successful" does not make them more or less gifted, creative, or talented. On the other hand, when and if they choose success for themselves, they can then own that success with the full knowledge that it came from them and not from you, and you can rest assured that you gave them support and permission to make that choice and see it through.

- Be watchful for signs that your child is fearful of displeasing you at the expense of knowing her own needs and desires. If your child is a habitual people pleaser, offer opportunities for her to go against your wishes without losing your love or respect.

- Think about aspects of your own schooling and childhood that might be influencing the choices you make with your children. Were there areas in which your parents did not support you and your intellectual or social and emotional needs? Are you over-compensating now with your own children? Are you sensitive to your children's needs? Spend some time thinking or writing about how your children's needs might be different from what your needs were.

- Take the time to learn about your own giftedness, intensities, talents, goals, and dreams. Make a commitment to meeting your own needs today as a gifted adult. How will you achieve this? When will you make time for your own needs?

- Listen to how you talk to others about your teenager's education, achievement, and plans, especially the college application process. Parents of gifted children often feel understandably frustrated because they have few people with whom they can talk honestly about their joys and challenges. However, if you hear yourself recounting "our" college search or where "we" are applying to college, or if you find yourself often mentioning your child's SAT scores or GPA or even IQ scores with people other than close family members and friends, it's time to step back a bit and reflect. What fears or hopes do those words reflect? How can we choose different words that will give our children the courage to live their own lives? How does sharing specific information about our children's accomplishments define our children—in ways we cannot control—both in their own minds and in the minds of others?

- Resist the urge to think of parenting in terms of good or bad, perfect or flawed. Sometimes teenagers make bad decisions that we simply cannot control, such as purposefully failing classes, shoplifting, or experimenting with drugs or alcohol. How we handle these situations as a family is what counts. Parents show love by setting boundaries when necessary. When we remove driving privileges when a teen cuts classes, refuse to lie to protect the consequences of a child's stealing, and insist on intervention and professional help for addictive behaviors, we are doing the hard but right thing for our families and for ourselves. Parents also show love by seeking professional counseling and medical and psychological services for themselves or their teens when problems become too big or too dangerous to handle on our own. Engaging in self-blame, on the other hand, helps no one. As parents, we do the best we can with the knowledge and skills we have at the time, which is why it is important to continue to learn and develop not only as parents, but as human beings. In that light, we can also be sure to forgive ourselves for any choices or actions that we may now regret.

> *My younger sister often feels that she has to copy my achievements. She sometimes shouts, "Just because you get straight A's doesn't mean I have to get them!" I understand the pressure she feels, but I can't go overboard over it because I think she's cheating herself. She's bright, too, but she's lazy. The thing of it is, in our house, it's normal to be ahead of yourself—we all are, or have been, including my parents.* (AAGC, 1978, p. 44)

Recommended Further Reading

The Highly Sensitive Person: How to Thrive when the World Over-whelms You
By Elaine Aron
Replica Books, 1999
Elaine Aron not only explains what it's like to be a highly sensitive person, but she also helps adults understand the role that sensitivity played in their childhoods and adolescence.

Life in the Fast Brain: Keeping Up with Gifted Minds
By Karen Isaacson
Great Potential Press, 2007
When the intensity of parenting gifted children seems overwhelming, read this humorous collection of real-life stories from a mother of five gifted children.

The Gifted Adult: A Revolutionary Guide for Liberating Everyday Genius
By Mary Elaine Jacobsen
Ballantine Books, 2000
Jacobsen offers advice for how adults can understand their "First Nature" traits of heightened receptivity and an urge to perfect—traits that gifted people are born with rather than are acquired—and how to manage the "Big Three" differences of intensity, complexity, and drive.

Dabrowski's Theory of Positive Disintegration
Edited by Sal Mendaglio
Great Potential Press, 2008
This collection of essays is a valuable resource for anyone who wants a deeper understanding of Dabrowski's theory. Some of the topics are creativity, authentic mental health, and authentic education.

In the Mind's Eye: Creative Visual Thinkers, Gifted Dyslexics, and the Rise of Visual Technologies
By Thomas G. West
Prometheus Books, 2nd edition, 2009
This revision of Thomas West's classic book offers a bold and exciting perspective on people who learn differently from the norm, especially dyslexics and creative learners.

Chapter 9
Conclusion:
Worry, Expectations, and Forgiveness

W e made it!

This was the shared feeling of families in our homeschooling group whose children were preparing to go to college in the fall. While our teens gathered for their regular *Star Trek* nights—sharing pizza and laughs and science fiction re-runs—we parents sat back, watched them, and marveled that we had somehow navigated the waters of curriculum, socializing, transcripts, college applications and acceptances, and yes, hormones.

Of course, in an important way, this was a new beginning and not the end. Our worries as parents were certainly not over. They had just changed from "How will I help my child with algebra homework?" and "Will my child be able to get into his first choice college?" and "What is the right college, anyway?" to "What gaps does my child have?" and "Will my child be able to handle a college schedule and make new friends?"

Worry[1]

From first words to toilet training. Reading. Learning to ride a two wheeler. Manners. Patience. Penmanship. Multiplication tables. Spelling. Fitting in. Being oneself. Following rules. Standing up for oneself. Computer time. Driving. Physical fitness. Studying. Time management. Dating. College preparation. Healthy eating. College applications. Living in a dorm.

If the above list makes your stomach turn or knot, you must be a parent. We parents worry about whether our children are learning enough, doing things on time, gaining needed skills, and generally becoming prepared for whatever life throws at them. We are wired to worry from the very beginning, when our baby's height and weight are charted according to percentiles and when we watch for and record the month and day our child first rolls over or smiles or crawls. We worry about various kinds of readiness: kindergarten readiness, reading readiness, sleepover readiness, dating readiness, college readiness.

As we've seen in earlier chapters, parents of gifted children also worry about other things: uneven development, levels of challenge, acceleration, finding friends, underachievement, and perfectionism. Even if our children are "on time" with skills, we worry that they should be doing them sooner because they are, after all, gifted. And if they are ahead of schedule, we worry that we are pushing them or that they aren't adequately challenged or that something else must need fixing.

Our answer to all of this worry is often to try to cram as much wisdom, skill, and experience into our children as possible in the years during which they are in our care. We are always thinking ahead, planning for what our children will need for the next step, helping them to improve. During adolescence, our worries, fears, and cramming escalate as we see the day they leave the nest looming ever closer.

With the best of intentions, in all this worry, could we be denying our children the courage to live their own lives? In the interim, are we losing sight of the joy of the moment as we look ahead, always to the future?

We naturally want to protect our children from pain. We remember life lessons that we learned the hard way, and we want to give our children the gift of our experience and wisdom. We read about the potential social and emotional minefields that our children may fall victim to, and we understandably feel that being a good parent means doing the work of finding and removing or avoiding those minefields, directing our children down a different path, away from danger.

Life, however, often throws us surprises.

Rethinking Expectations

Now that our son is 18, I sometimes think back to the worries and expectations I had as he was growing up. Some of them were academic in nature: learning multiplication tables, writing in cursive, fitting in lab science as a homeschooler. Others had to do with social-emotional needs: balancing alone time with social time, finding good friends, fostering self-confidence, figuring out his life's work and calling.

Most of my worries were a waste of time. He learned multiplication simultaneously when he learned algebra. He never did learn cursive, except for his signature, and probably will never need it. I know from experience that a small fraction of college students write anything in cursive (and if our son does need cursive skills or wants to learn them, he can pick them up fast). He skipped high school lab science altogether and instead took a college chemistry class when he was 15. His passion was not in math or science, but in history and literature.

In terms of finding a good balance of alone time and social time, this need continues to change as he now lives in a college dorm, and I've learned to trust that he'll figure it out along the way and ask for help and advice when he needs it. Through a theater program and our home-schooling group, he has a group of very close friends that he keeps in touch with—both boys and girls—better friends than I ever had at his age. When he was seven or even 10, I could not have foreseen this gift in his life. His self-confidence and self-knowledge continue to grow, and I frequently remind myself that as much as I'd like to, I can't see the world through his eyes. His perspective is his own, and rightly so.

Even his interests have surprised me throughout the years. Not until the summer before his senior high school year did he show what has become a consuming passion that, for now, seems as though it may become his eventual career: public policy. The election of 2008 triggered a synthesis of interests that he had all along—history, philosophy, language arts—but the separate areas hadn't yet come together. Just as he once immersed himself in Peanuts comics until he knew every literature reference and all of the changes that occurred in the five decades during which the strip was produced, he was now keeping up with all of the major news sources and blogs from many different political perspectives and educating himself on how our government works and who the voices are that shape domestic and foreign policy. Had he entered college at an earlier age, I am convinced that he would have had neither the time nor the opportunity for this passion to develop, and I am grateful that he never lost the ability to direct (and to trust) his own learning and to lose himself in the joy of deep discovery.

The experience of homeschoolers offers all of us valuable insights into what is necessary in education, especially for intense, asynchronous, and driven children whose learning fiercely resists any one-size-fits-all templates. We mistakenly assume that specific subjects need to be learned in specific grades (they don't), that review of last year's material is always necessary at the beginning of each school year (it isn't), or that gaps in knowledge cannot be addressed later (they can).

The next time you find yourself worrying excessively about an expectation that your child or teenager is not meeting, ask yourself this: What if that expectation were not met until later? How might things still work out? What if she needs to learn this skill on her own? How much of your expectation is based on either what others think or what you assume gifted children should be doing? What if you decide not to worry about it just for today and to enjoy your family just as it is, to play in the sunshine (or rain or snow)?

The Power of Forgiveness

As parents learn about their children's giftedness and perhaps their own, they might at times be overcome with feelings of regret, self-blame, and even anger—anger at how they were misunderstood as children, regret for lost years when they did not understand their own gifted differences, self-blame and guilt for ways in which they have not understood or addressed their own children's needs.

To that end, I'd like to share my own journey toward understanding and forgiveness, in case it strikes a chord with other readers. In my forties as I write this, I am now for the first time experiencing the joy of being organized. I will never have the orderly life of the people I know who are natural filers (rather than pilers). However, I have learned, finally, to break big tasks and goals into small steps, to congratulate myself for whatever steps I do take, to make lists, to meet deadlines, and to take better control of my time.

This is in stark contrast to my previous habits. My mother, highly creative and artistic, did not have strong organization skills while I was young, although she did develop them, as I have, in her forties. As a young girl, I remember wishing I had the kind of mother who made chore charts and schedules and whose house was spotless with clothes neatly pressed. I thought that if *she* were more organized, I would be, too.

It didn't help that I didn't need skills of time management or organization to do well in school. The expectations of the teachers were low, and I didn't push myself to go beyond them. In college, I hit a wall of sorts, receiving grades lower than A's for the first time. I somehow learned to cram more effectively and even once in awhile to write more than one draft of a paper. However, I can't say that I ever developed habits of organization or good study skills. I don't like to feel boxed in by too many rules or deadlines, and I have a high tolerance for disorder.

This is not all bad. My openness and acceptance of the messier parts of life are part of what has made unschooling (child-directed learning) work so well for our family. At the same time, though, I was continually frustrated with never meeting personal goals and feeling that my life was slipping away from me. I also was beginning to see just how much I dislike the feeling of being overwhelmed.

So what has now changed for me?

In the years leading up to our son's going to college, I spent a lot of time thinking about making the transition from a homeschooling parent to an empty nester. I love my freelance work (writing and indexing), researching, and teaching. The "lightbulb" moment for me was when I realized that I love my work even more and do it even better when I am on top of things. Who would have thought that being disorganized and not taking control of my time make me less—not more—creative?! Or that adding some aspects of organization and self-discipline to my life does not take away from my ability to go with the flow or become immersed in the moment? If I can be even more creative and joyful with a little bit of organization, it's worth the effort to spend some time toward organization.

You might be thinking that it would have been better for my mother to have taught me these lessons earlier—that my learning them on my own points to wasted years and lost potential. I thought that way, too, for a long time, blaming her for not being a more hands-on, involved parent.

The reality, however, is that my mother was exactly the kind of mother I needed. She passed away (far too young at age 56 from multiple myeloma), but in the last 15 years of her life, she found herself and her passions and reinvented herself. She formed her own quilting business, saving money a little at time until she could buy her own long-arm quilting machine. She published a newsletter devoted to long-arm quilting. She designed and sold patchwork patterns and quilting stitches, and she did mail-order work for people all across the country, including Alaska. Somehow, from this work and the need it fulfilled, grew the skills that she needed to be a business woman and a working artist—all from a farmhouse in the seventh poorest county in the nation. She hired a weekly cleaning woman, told my dad he could get his own lunch once in awhile, and got her life and time in order. She took control.

Who am I kidding? Had she been the mother I *thought* I needed, using charts and schedules and lists to try to *make* me organized, I would have rebelled (I was that kind of kid). I needed—*demanded*—my mental and physical space. My mother, with her intuition and her own tolerance for letting others go their own way, met this need, and for that I am forever grateful. Now I am learning these new skills for myself, for how I want to feel and live, and just when I need them most. I only wish I had reached this understanding and forgiveness in time to tell her "thank you" for letting me be who I am and grow up in my own way.

The goals of self-management, lifelong learning, growth, and self-actualization—rather than parenting primarily for early public success and high achievement—remove many of the artificial timetables that we impose on ourselves and our children. Our children ultimately will make mistakes, learn from them, and be in control of their lives. They (and we) will never run out of things to learn about our world and ourselves.

How we change and grow as adults, right in front of our children, where they can see us, is more effective in the long run than cajoling and nagging and bribing and, yes, worrying about expectations that may not be realistic. In his last years of high school, I watched with interest as my son, on his own, became much more organized: using his white board to make lists, giving himself points for getting tasks done during the day, and asking for reminders when he needed them without accusing us of nagging him (parents of teenagers all surely know what a breakthrough this is!). I don't think it is coincidence that this change in him happened only after I began to change myself.

When we choose to understand and forgive not only our parents and teachers, but ourselves for acting on incomplete knowledge, we open doors to present and future growth and happiness that are otherwise closed. Are there areas of your past that you need to forgive and release? Perhaps your parents didn't recognize or support your accomplishments because they didn't want you to get a "big head." Perhaps your school didn't offer enough challenge to keep you from being bored, and you failed to develop good study skills. Perhaps classmates ridiculed you for your intensity and sensitivity. Maybe you experienced unusual stress due to divorce or other difficult situations in the family, and it affected your ability to trust a relationship with the opposite sex. Now is the time to acknowledge your feelings of hurt and anger, then recognize that they are in the past and cannot hurt you today unless you let them. Today you can move on.

Here is another story of forgiveness, this time forgiveness of self. When our son was in preschool, he cried nearly every day when I picked him up at noon. This was well before I was introduced to the ideas of giftedness and an understanding of possible causes of his behaviors. All I knew was that the other children weren't crying, the other parents were looking at me in ways I saw as judgmental, and the preschool teachers were beginning to express concerns which implied that our son might have attachment issues.

Not until years later, after seeing him in similar situations and learning more about intensity and excitabilities, did I realize that all I would have needed to do while I helped him with his coat and boots was take him into the nearby hall, which was quiet and empty. There, away from the noise and the bustle and the smells of snack bags, he would have been able to relax and tolerate better the transition from preschool to home.

The fact that I so vividly recall those mornings full of tension shows how much I replayed them in my mind—thinking about and regretting them. It took awhile for me to realize that there is no way I could have known why he was reacting as he did, and his teachers weren't well-versed in giftedness to pick up on the clues. The only thing I could do was forgive myself and make new choices with the knowledge I continued to gather.

This is why it is so important to resist the elitist charge against the very idea of giftedness. When parents and teachers ignore the gifted difference, when they use the misguided mantra of "every child is gifted" as a way to shut their minds to the real challenges and extremes experienced by unusually bright, intense, and sensitive children, we all suffer, because those children are not only less likely to be accepted for who they are, they are also less likely to understand and accept themselves and less likely to go out into the world and take their rightful place alongside everyone else.

In terms of summing up the gift that we can give our intense, gifted children, I can think of no better words than these, which Eleanor Roosevelt wrote in 1941 in a letter to a friend:

> *Somewhere along the line of development we discover what we really are and then make our real decision for which we are responsible. Make that decision primarily for yourself because you can never really live anyone else's life, not even your child's. The influence you exert is through your own life and what you become yourself.*[2]

Endnotes

Chapter 1

1   Roeper, 1996, p. 18

2   Roeper, 2007, p. 92

3   Roeper, 1990, p. 5

4   Roeper, 2007, p. 94

5   Csikszentmihalyi, 1998

6   Arnold, 1995, p. 41

7   Arnold, 1995, p. 42

8   Fredericks, Alfeld, & Eccles, 2010

9   Apter, 2002, p. 55

10 J. T. Webb, 2007, p. 15

11 J. T. Webb, 2007. p. 4

12 American Association for Gifted Children, 1978

Chapter 2

1   Csikszentmihalyi, Rathunde, & Whalen, 1993, p. 149

2   See, for example, state gifted and talented definitions, Education Commission of the States (ECS), at www.ecs.org/clearinghouse/52/28/5228.htm.

3   Retrieved January 26, 2010, from www.nagc.org

4   www.nagc.org

5   www.nagc.org

6   www.nagc.org

7   Morelock, 1996, p. 8

8   Jacobsen, 2000

9   Jacobsen, 2003

10 Jacobsen, 2000

11 Adapted by permission of Annemarie Roeper from www.roeperconsultation.net/characteristics.htm.

12 Jean Piaget's theory of cognitive development states that stages of intellectual growth—preoperational, concrete operational, and formal operational—are unalterable in their sequence, and he poses that abstract and hypothetical thinking are possible only in the last, formal operational stage, which begins at about age 11. For a discussion of Piaget's stages as they relate to giftedness, see Dixon (2007).

13 Ruf, 2009

14 Csikszentmihalyi et al., 1993, p. 23

15 Robinson, 2009

16 Parents who want a more detailed discussion and a bit of a different perspective on the definitions of "giftedness" and "talent" can read the chapter "What Kind of Gifted Children Do You Have" in Karen Rogers' book *Re-Forming Gifted Education: How Parents and Teachers Can Match the Program to the Child* (Great Potential Press, 2002), especially the section "Not All Gifts Become Talents," pp. 32-35.

17 Gladwell, 2008, p. 38

18 Gladwell, 2008, p. 39

19 Dweck, 2007, p. 6

20 Dweck, 2007, p. 7

21 U.S. Department of Education, 1993

22 Robinson, 2009

23 Csikszentmihalyi et al., 1993, p. 148

24 *Is success linked to talent?*, 2009

25 Dweck, 2007, p. 179

26 Robinson, 2009, pp., 11, 228

27 Piirto, 2004, p. 452

28 Lovecky, 1992, p. 19

29 Csikszentmihalyi, 1997, pp. 60-61

30 Lovecky, 1992, p. 19

31 Csikzentmihalyi, 1997

32 Black, 1998, p. 2

33 Winner, 1997

34 VanTassel-Baska, 2004

Chapter 3

1 Duncan, 2009

2 Public Broadcasting Service, 2009

3 Daniels & Piechowski, 2009, p. 9

4 Piechowski, 2006, p. 17

5 Webb, Gore, Amend, & DeVries, 2007, p. 22

6   Adapted and reprinted with permission from Michael M. Piechowski (Piechowski, 2006).

7   Webb, 2008

8   Tillier, 2009, pp. 124-5

9   Jackson & Moyle, 2009, p. 58

10 H. Voss, personal communication, August 9, 2008

11 Willis, 2009

12 Winner, 1997, pp. 3-4

13 Piechowski, 2006, p. 69

14 Piirto, 2004, p. 61

15 Goertzel, Goertzel, Goertzel, & Hansen, 2004, p. 353

16 Piechowski, 2006

17 Tolan, 2007

18 Csikszentmihalyi et al., 1993

19 www.roeperconsultation.net/characteristics.htm

20 Sheely, 2000

21 www.talentdevelop.com/articles/sexhighlygftd.html

22 Sheely, 2000

23 Webb et al., 2004, p. 229; Piirto, 2004, pp. 116-18

24 Daniels, 2009, p. 129

25 Daniels, 2009, p. 144

26 For information about counseling for the gifted, see www.hoagiesgifted.org/counseling.htm.

27 Henig, 2009

Chapter 4

1   Jackson & Peterson, 2003, p. 178

2   Roeper, 2003

3   Whitmer, n.d.

4   Whitmer, n.d.

5   Winerip, 2007

6   Kaufman, 1992

7   Kaufman, 1992

8   Kaufman, 1981

9   Kaufman, 1992

10 Kaufman, 1992

11 Kaufman, 1992

12 List adapted from Jackson & Moyle (2009, pp. 68-9)

13 Apter, 2002, p. 29

14 Restak, 2006; Willis, 2009, p. 50

15 Clark, 2008, p. 146

16 Webb et al., 2004

17 Many of the suggestions for parents in this chapter are based on Lovecky (1992).

18 J. T. Webb, 2007

19 Bronson, 2007

20 Lamberg, 2009

21 Bronson, 2007

22 Lind, 2003

23 Retrieved October 16, 2009, from http://dictionary.reference.com/browse/anxious

24 Shani, 2009

25 Silverman, 2009

26 Laney, 2005, p. 14

27 Silverman, 1988

28 Silverman, 1988, p. 11

29 Gray, 2008

30 Clark, 2008, p. 117

31 Csikszentmihalyi et al., 1993, p. 91

32 Edmunds & Edmunds, 2005, p. 77

Chapter 5

1   Torrance, 1963, p. 137-8

2   Whitmore, 1980

3   Webb et al., 2005, p. 41

4   Torrance & Goff, 1990

5   "11001001," 1988 episode of Star Trek: The Next Generation (1987-94; Paramount, 2008 DVD)

6   Palladino, 1999, pp. 21-2

7   Webb et al., 2005

8   Cropley, 2006

9   Cropley, 2006, p. 402

10 Csikszentmihalyi, 1997, p. 362

11 Adapted from Csikszentmihalyi (1997)

12 Csikszentmihalyi, 1997 p. 60

13 Csikszentmihalyi et al., 1993, p. 253

14 Adapted from Csikszentmihalyi (1997)

15 Csikszentmihalyi, 1997, p. 107

16 Csikszentmihalyi et al., 1993, p. 248

17 Csikszentmihalyi et al., 1993, p. 247

18 Many effective and fun creative thinking activities are available for free on the Web. Search for "creative thinking exercises" or "creative thinking activities." Jane Piirto's book *Understanding Creativity* (2004) and Edward de Bono's books on lateral thinking also contain many family-friendly ideas.

19 Schrok, 2009

20 Amabile, 1989

21 Dweck, 2007

22 de Bono, 1993

Chapter 6

1 Lovecky, 1992, p. 24

2 Lovecky, 1986

3 Jacobsen, 2000, pp. 39-40

4 Jacobsen, 2000, p. 284

5 Kohl, 1991, p. 13

6 Kohl, 1991, p. 17

7 Kohl, 1991, p. 16

8 Willis, 2009, p. 50

9 I am grateful to Janet Gore and Dr. Nadia Webb for their help in understanding and explaining the brain maturation process.

10 Willis, 2009, p. 50

11 Willis, 2009, p. 48

12 N. Webb, 2007

13 N. Webb, 2007

14 Lowry, 1989

15 Adapted from Lowry (1989)

16 Betts & Kercher, 1999, p. 14

17 Freeman, 1985

18 Lowry, 1989

19 Willis, 2009

20 Csikszentmihalyi, 1998

21 Webb et al., 2005

22 Lovecky, 2004, p. 23

23 Webb, 2008

Chapter 7

1   Lovecky, 2004, p. 24

2   Webb, 2008

3   Achter, Lubinski, & Benbow, 1996, p. 73

4   Robinson, 2009

5   Robinson, 2009, p. 21

6   Achter, Lubinski, & Benbow, 1996

7   Achter et al., 1996

8   Arnold, 1995, p. 284

9   U.S. Department of Labor, Bureau of Labor Statistics, 2008

10 Greene, 2005

Chapter 8

1   Jacobsen, 2000, p. 17

2   Mendaglio, 2008, pp. 24-5

3   Mendaglio, 2008, p. 24

4   Webb, 2008

5   Jacobsen, 2000

6   The following lists are taken from Jacobsen, 2000, pp. 259-60.

7   Johnson & Eskelsen, 2006, p. 213

8   The "urge to perfect" is one of Jacobsen's (2000) First Nature traits of giftedness. First Nature traits are traits that gifted people are born with or that are "hard wired" rather than acquired.

Chapter 9

1   Portions of this chapter were originally published on the Gifted Homeschoolers Forum website: http://giftedhomeschoolers.org/articles/unnecessary.html

2   Wigal, 2003, p. 29

References

Achter, J. A., Lubinski, D., & Benbow, C. P. (1996). Multipotentiality among intellectually gifted: It was never there and already it's vanishing. *Journal of Counseling Psychology, 43,* 65-76.

Amabile, T. (1989). *Growing up creative: Nurturing a lifetime of creativity.* New York: Crown.

American Association for Gifted Children. (1978). *On being gifted.* New York: Walker & Co.

Apter, T. (2002). *The myth of maturity: What teenagers need from parents to become adults.* New York: Norton.

Arnold, K. D. (1995). *Lives of promise: What becomes of high school valedictorians.* San Francisco: Jossey-Bass.

Betts, G. T., & Kercher, J. K. (1999). *The autonomous learner model: Optimizing ability.* Greeley, CO: ALPS.

Black, R. A. (1998). *Broken crayons: Break your crayons and draw outside the lines.* Athens, GA: Cre8ng Places Press.

Bronson, P. (2007, Oct. 7). Snooze or lose? *New York Magazine.* Retrieved October 29, 2009, from nymag.com/news/features/38951

Clark, B. (2008). *Growing up gifted: Developing the potential of children at home and at school* (7th ed.). Upper Saddle River, NJ: Pearson/Merrill Prentice Hall.

Cropley, A. (2006). In praise of convergent thinking. *Creativity Research Journal, 18*(3), 391-404.

Csikszentmihalyi, M. (1997). *Creativity: Flow and the psychology of discovery and invention.* New York: Harper Perennial.

Csikszentmihalyi, M. (1998). *Finding flow: The psychology of engagement with everyday life.* New York: Basic Books.

Csikszentmihalyi, M., Rathunde, K., & Whalen, S. (1993). *Talented teenagers: The roots of success and failure.* New York: Cambridge University Press.

Daniels, S. (2009). Overexcitability, giftedness, and family dynamics. In S. Daniels & M. M. Piechowski (Eds.), *Living with intensity: Understanding the sensitivity, excitability, and emotional development of gifted children, adolescents, and adults* (pp. 127-144). Scottsdale, AZ: Great Potential Press.

Daniels, S., & Piechowski, M. M. (2009). Embracing intensity, overexcitability, sensitivity, and the developmental potential of the gifted. In S. Daniels & M. M. Piechowski (Eds.), *Living with intensity: Understanding the sensitivity, excitability, and emotional development of gifted children, adolescents, and adults* (pp. 3-18). Scottsdale, AZ: Great Potential Press.

de Bono, E. (1993). *Serious creativity: Using the power of lateral thinking to create new ideas.* New York: HarperBusiness.

Dixon, F. A. (2007). Cognitive development. In J. A. Plucker & C. M. Callahan (Eds.), *Critical issues and practices in gifted education: What the research says* (pp. 85-95). Waco, TX: Prufrock Press.

Duncan, D. (2009). *The national parks: America's best idea* [television documentary]. Public Broadcasting Service.

Dweck, C. (2007). *Mindset: The new psychology of success.* New York: Ballantine Books.

Edmunds, A. L., & Edmunds, G. (2005). Sensitivity: A double-edged sword for the pre-adolescent and adolescent gifted child. *Roeper Review, 27*(2), 69-77.

Fredricks, J. A., Alfeld, C., & Eccles, J. (2010). Developing and fostering passion in academic and nonacademic domains. *Gifted Child Quarterly, 54*(1), 18-30.

Freeman, J. (1985). A pedagogy for the gifted. In J. Freeman (Ed.), *The psychology of gifted children: Perspectives on development and education* (pp. 1-20). New York: Wiley.

Gladwell, M. (2008). *Outliers: The story of success.* New York: Little, Brown & Co.

Goertzel, M. G., Goertzel, V., Goertzel, T. G., & Hansen, A. M. W. (2004). *Cradles of eminence: Childhoods of more than 700 famous men and women.* Scottsdale, AZ: Great Potential Press.

Gray, P. (2008, Sept. 9).Why we should stop segregating children by age: Part I—The value of play in the zone of proximal development. *Psychology Today.* Retrieved October 29, 2009, from www.psychologytoday.com/blog/freedom-learn/200809/why-we-should-stop-segregating-children-age-part-i-the-value-play-in-the-z

Greene, M. J. (2005).Multipotentiality: Issues and considerations for career planning. *Duke Gifted Letter, 6*(1). Retrieved October 29, 2009, from www.dukegiftedletter.com/articles/vol6no1_feature.html

Henig, M. (2009, Sept. 29). Understanding the anxious mind. *New York Times.* Retrieved October 29, 2009, from www.nytimes.com/2009/10/04/magazine/04anxiety-t.html

Is success linked to talent? (2009, April 12). [On *Global Public Square* (television news program)]. Retrieved January 19, 2010 from http://transcripts.cnn.com/TRANSCRIPTS/0904/12/fzgps.01.html

Jackson, S., & Moyle, V. F. (2009). Inner awakening, outward journey: The intense gifted child in adolescence. In S. Daniels & M. M. Piechowski (Eds.), *Living with intensity: Understanding the sensitivity, excitability, and emotional development of gifted children, adolescents, and adults* (pp. 57–72). Scottsdale, AZ: Great Potential Press.

Jackson, S., & Peterson, J. (2003). Depressive disorder in highly gifted adolescents. *The Journal of Secondary Gifted Education, 14*(3), 175–186.

Jacobsen, M. E. (2000). *The gifted adult: A revolutionary guide for liberating everyday genius.* New York: Ballantine Books.

Jacobsen, M. E. (2003). *Tips for parents: The real world of gifted teens.* Retrieved October 28, 2009, from www.davidsongifted.org/db/Articles_id_10250.aspx

Johnson, N., & Eskelsen, E. (2006). *Conquering the SAT: How parents can help teens overcome the pressure and succeed.* New York: Palgrave Macmillan.

Kaufman, F. (1981). *The 1964-1968 Presidential Scholars: A follow-up study.* Retrieved November 26, 2009, from www.davidsongifted.org/db/Articles_id_10078.aspx

Kaufman, F. (1992). *What educators can learn from gifted adults.* Retrieved November 26, 2009, from www.davidsongifted.org/db/Articles_id_10023.aspx

Kohl, H. (1991). *"I won't learn from you" and other thoughts on creative maladjustment.* Minneapolis, MN: Milkweed.

Lamberg, L. (2009, June 3). High schools find later start time helps students' health and performance. *Journal of the American Medical Association, 301*(21), 2200–2201.

Laney, M. O. (2005). *The hidden gifts of the introverted child: Helping your child thrive in an extroverted world.* New York: Workman.

Lind, S. (2003). *Tips for parents: Developing a feeling vocabulary.* Retrieved October 29, 2009, from www.davidsongifted.org/db/Articles_id_10233.aspx

Lovecky, D. (1986, May). Can you hear the flowers sing? Issues for gifted adults. *Journal of Counseling and Development, 64*(9), 572–575.

Lovecky, D. (1992). Exploring social and emotional aspects of giftedness in children. *Roeper Review, 15*(1), 18–25.

Lovecky, D. (2004). *Different minds: Gifted children with AD/HD, Asperger Syndrome, and other learning deficits.* London: Jessica Kingsley.

Lowry, C. M. (1989). *Supporting and facilitating self-directed learning.* Retrieved January 26, 2010, from http://search.ebscohost.com/login.aspx?direct=true&db=eric&AN=ED312457&loginpage=Login.asp&site=ehost-live (ERIC database; ED312457).

Mendaglio, S. (2008). Dabrowski's theory of positive disintegration: A personality theory for the 21st century. In S. Mendaglio (Ed.), *Dabrowski's theory of positive disintegration* (pp. 13-40). Scottsdale, AZ: Great Potential Press.

Morelock, M. J. (1996). On the nature of giftedness and talent: Imposing order on chaos. *Roeper Review, 19*(1), 4-12.

Palladino, L. J. (1999). *Dreamers, discoverers & dynamos: How to help the child who is bright, bored and having problems in school.* New York: Ballantine Books.

Piechowski, M. (2006). *"Mellow out," they say. If I only could: Intensities and sensitivities of the young and bright.* Madison, WI: Yunasa Books.

Piirto, J. (2004). *Understanding creativity.* Scottsdale, AZ: Great Potential Press.

Public Broadcasting Service. (2009). *Q & A with Dayton Duncan.* Retrieved October 29, 2009, from www.pbs.org/nationalparks/about/qa-dayton-duncan

Restak, R. (2006). *The naked brain: How the emerging neurosociety is changing how we live, work, and love.* New York: Harmony.

Robinson, K. (2009). *The element: How finding your passion changes everything.* New York: Penguin.

Roeper, A. M. (1990). *Educating children for life: The modern learning community.* Monroe, NY: Trillium Press.

Roeper, A. M. (1996). A personal statement of philosophy of George and Annemarie Roeper. *Roeper Review, 19*(1), 18.

Roeper, A. M. (2003). *The emotional needs of the gifted child.* Retrieved October 29, 2009, from www.sengifted.org/articles_social/Roeper_TheEmotionalNeedsOfTheGiftedChild.shtml

Roeper, A. M. (2007). *The "I" of the beholder: A guided journey to the essence of a child.* Scottsdale, AZ: Great Potential Press.

Ruf, D. (2009). *5 Levels of gifted: School issues and educational options.* Scottsdale, AZ: Great Potential Press.

Schrok, K. (2009). *Imaginary worlds are early sign of highly creative kids.* Retrieved October 29, 2009, from www.scientificamerican.com/blog/60-second-science/post.cfm?id=imaginary-worlds-are-early-sign-of-2009-08-07

Shani, I. (2009, June 10). Gifted children shape their personalities according to social stigma. *ScienceDaily.* Retrieved October 29, 2009, from www.sciencedaily.com/releases/2009/03/090303102614.htm#

Sheely, A. R. (2000). Sex and the highly gifted adolescent. *Highly Gifted Children Newsletter, 13*(2), 30-33. Also available at http://talentdevelop.com/articles/sexhighlygftd.html

Silber, L. (2004). *Organizing from the right side of the brain: A creative approach to getting organized.* New York: St. Martin's Griffin.

Silverman, L. K. (1988, Nov. 10). Personality plus: On introversion. *Understanding Our Gifted, 1*(2), 11.

Silverman, L. K. (2009). *What we have learned about gifted children.* Retrieved November 4, 2009, from www.gifteddevelopment.com/What_is_Gifted/learned.htm

Tillier, W. (2009). Dabrowski without the theory of positive disintegration just isn't Dabrowski. *Roeper Review, 31*(2), 123-126.

Tolan, S. (2007). *Sex and the highly gifted adolescent.* Retrieved November 26, 2009, from www.stephanietolan.com/hg_adolescent.htm

Torrance, E. P. (1963). Toward the more humane education of gifted children. *Gifted Child Quarterly, 7*(4), 135-145.

Torrance, E. P., & Goff, K. (1990). *Fostering academic creativity in gifted students.* Retrieved January 26, 2010, from http://search.ebscohost.com/login.aspx?direct=true&db=eric&AN=ED321489&loginpage=Login.asp&site=ehost-live (ERIC database; ED321489).

U.S. Department of Education. (1993). *National excellence: A case for developing America's talent.* Washington, DC: Office of Educational Research and Improvement.

U.S. Department of Labor, Bureau of Labor Statistics. (2008, June). *Number of jobs held, labor market activity, and earnings growth among the youngest baby boomers: Results from a longitudinal survey.* Retrieved October 29, 2009, from www.bls.gov/news.release/pdf/nlsoy.pdf

VanTassel-Baska, J. (2004). *Creativity as an elusive factor in giftedness.* Retrieved October 28, 2009, from www.cfge.wm.edu/Gifted%20Educ%20Artices/Creativity.html

Webb, J. T. (2007, July). *Cultivating courage, creativity, and caring.* Paper presented at the 24th Annual SENG Conference, Kansas City/Overland Park, Kansas.

Webb, J. T. (2008). *Dabrowski's theory and existential depression in gifted children and adults.* Retrieved October 29, 2009, from www.davidsongifted.org/db/Articles_id_10554.aspx

Webb, J. T., Amend, E. R., Webb, N. E., Goerss, J., Beljan, P., & Olenchak, F. R. (2004). *Misdiagnosis and dual diagnosis of gifted children.* Retrieved October 29, 2009, from www.sengifted.org/articles_counseling/Webb_ MisdiagnosisAndDualDiagnosisOfGiftedChildren.shtml

Webb, J. T., Amend, E. R., Webb, N. E., Goerss, J., Beljan, P., & Olenchak, F. R. (2005). *Misdiagnosis and dual diagnoses of gifted children and adults: ADHD, bipolar, OCD, Asperger's, depression, and other disorders.* Scottsdale, AZ: Great Potential Press.

Webb, J. T., Gore, J. L., Amend, E. R., & DeVries, A. R. (2007). *A parent's guide to gifted children*. Scottsdale, AZ: Great Potential Press.

Webb, N. (2007). *Tips for parents: Surviving your gifted teen*. Retrieved October 29, 2009, from www.davidsongifted.org/db/Articles_id_10408.aspx

Whitmer, B. (n.d.). *College prep: One mom's timeline for high school*. Retrieved October 29, 2009, from www.greatschools.net/college-prep/planning/one-moms-timeline.gs?content=580&page=1

Whitmore, J. (1980). *Giftedness, conflict, and underachievement*. New York: Allyn & Bacon.

Wigal, D. (Ed.). (2003). *The wisdom of Eleanor Roosevelt*. New York: Kensington Press.

Willis, J. A. (2009). *Inspiring middle school minds: Gifted, creative, and challenging*. Scottsdale, AZ: Great Potential Press.

Winerip, M. (2007, April 29). Young, gifted, and not getting into Harvard. *New York Times*. Retrieved October 29, 2009, from www.nytimes.com/2007/04/29/nyregion/nyregionspecial2/29Rparenting.html?_r=1

Winner, E. (1997). *Gifted children: Myths and realities*. New York: Basic Books.

Index

About the Author

Lisa Rivero lives in Milwaukee, Wisconsin, where she is a writer, teacher, speaker, and parent. She has taught and mentored teens at the middle school, high school, and college levels, and she always enjoys helping young people to discover, appreciate, and use their creativity, drive, passion, and love of learning. She currently teaches at the Milwaukee School of Engineering, and she is a board member of SENG (Supporting Emotional Needs of the Gifted), a national nonprofit organization.

Lisa's articles have appeared in several national publications, among which are *Parenting for High Potential*, *Duke Gifted Letter*, *Roeper Review*, and *Understanding Our Gifted*. Her other books include the award-winning *Creative Home Schooling: A Resource Guide for Smart Families* (2003 Glyph Best Education Book Award); *Gifted Education at Home: A Case for Self-Directed Homeschooling*; *The Homeschooling Option: How to Decide When It Is Right for Your Family*; and *The Smart Teens' Guide to Living with Intensity: How to Get More Out of Life and Learning*. She speaks at state and national conferences on issues of giftedness, homeschooling, and creativity.